THE SHORT SALE SAVIOR

"No need to stress out about the mortgage you can't afford and the house you can't unload! The Short Sale Savior gives homeowners the answers and specific techniques to get it done."

—BARBARA CORCORAN
FOUNDER, THE CORCORAN GROUP

Every home owner and real estate investor should have a copy of The Short Sale Savior. Elizabeth Weintraub provides solid fundamentals and specific techniques to conduct a short sale.

—JOSEF KATZ
VICE PRESIDENT OF MARKETING, TRUMP UNIVERSITY

"Between her column on About.com and the valuable advice she offers on Trulia.com and on her blog, Elizabeth Weintraub has helped thousands of home buyers and sellers purchase or sell a short-sale property. The Short Sale Savior uses real-world examples and straightforward language to break down what can be an extremely complicated process. It's very informative and educational for anyone considering a short sale transaction."

—PETE FLINT, CEO, TRULIA.

THE SHORT SALE SAVIOR

TURNING YOUR UPSIDE-DOWN MORTGAGE RIGHT SIDE UP

ELIZABETH WEINTRAUB

ABOUT.COM REAL ESTATE EXPERT

 For information address Archer Ellison Publishing, P.O. Box 950696, Lake Mary, FL 32795

Archer Ellison Publishing books may be purchased for educational, business or sales promotional use. For information please write to: Special Sales Department, Archer Ellison, Inc. P.O. Box 950696, Lake Mary FL 32795

ISBN 13: 978-1-57472-376-2
Library of Congress Control Number: 2009923669

Visit TheShortSaleSavior.com for FREE Resources and to learn more about Elizabeth's in-depth Short Sale Savior home study course.

To all homeowners who are struggling...
may you find comfort in knowing
there is always something you can do
to improve your situation and your lives.

Contents

Introduction

We wanted to be the first, and we are, to release a book that helps homeowners who are underwater in their properties get their lives back on track. We felt it was important to release a book on the Short Sale that wasn't about greed. Until this book was published, unfortunately, all of the books on the Short Sale were written from the viewpoint that amateur real estate investors could get rich off of those who were underwater in their properties.

Here is our message to you:

If you find yourself in a challenging situation with your property, don't despair, you're not alone. It is our desire that The Short Sale Savior will not only give you hope, but will become a wellspring of knowledge that will help you improve your own situation.

We welcome you to visit TheShortSaleSavior.com for FREE Resources and to learn more about Elizabeth's in-depth Short Sale Savior home study course that includes all of the actual letters and forms you will need to get your short sale done in record time.

1

Overview of the Foreclosure Process

My mother grew up during the Great Depression when foreclosures were considered a stigma and avoided at all cost. People who lost their homes in foreclosures were ostracized, and others whispered about them. Today? Not so much.

Today, foreclosure is considered a viable option for many homeowners whose homes are underwater or for people who have hit a rough patch in life. Regardless, it is not a fun process, and I do not know anybody who looks forward to going through foreclosure.

The fact remains that if you do not make your mortgage payments, at some point, the lender will begin a foreclosure process to take away your home. There is a saying I like to tell first-time homebuyers when they ask what is contained in the bazillion pages of their mortgage documents. The 105 pages of loan documents one signs at closing boils down to this: *If you pay, you stay. If you don't, you won't.*

The Three Types of Foreclosure

Post-Foreclosure Stage

Let's start at the end and work our way back to the beginning. The very worst type of foreclosure for a homeowner is the post-foreclosure stage. This is, after all, when the time for redemption, meaning the right to reinstate the loan, has passed and when the lender has received and recorded formal title to the property. At this point, the home no longer belongs to you; it belongs to the bank.

Banks are not in the business of owning real estate. Banks are in the business of lending money to customers, using real estate as collateral for the loan, along with selling other financial products and services such as accepting funds from depositors and extending credit. Some of the bank's loans are unsecured and others are secured to automobiles or real estate used as collateral for the loan. Banks typically extend more credit than they have in cash on hand, which the Federal Reserve regulates. When a bank takes title to a home through a foreclosure process, the bank must sell that home to cut its losses.

The bank has already lost money at the post-foreclosure stage. For one thing, the bank has not received any payments for a while and has forever lost the potential to earn interest from those missed payments. For another, there are costs associated with filing a foreclosure, such as the fees to try to collect from the homeowner, the cost of initiating the foreclosure process (some states require the bank to pay the trustee's fee), not to mention the cost of the public auction, the publication expenses, and appraisal and recording fees.

If a bank carries too many repossessed homes on the books, that can affect its balance sheets. An REO (bank-owned home) is a liability to the bank. It is not an asset. When a bank's liabilities increase, consumer confidence decreases. When consumers lose confidence in a bank, they often withdraw their deposits. If too many people withdraw all their money from a bank, the bank may not have enough cash on hand to pay demands, which can result in what is called a "run on the bank." When banks do not maintain enough in deposits to satisfy the Federal Reserve requirements, the government might shut down the bank. This is not the only reason, though, why banks are eager to dispose of their post-foreclosure inventory.

You might be wondering how banks end up with post-foreclosure homes. The answer is nobody bid enough at the auction to outbid the bank. The bank's opening bid is normally the amount of money that is owed to the bank.

When the bank has received title to a home in foreclosure, the bank has several ways to sell the home. It can offer the home for sale directly from the bank. You can find Web sites where banks will list inventory of REOs for sale. Often, though, the bank will list the home with a local real estate agent who specializes in selling REOs. Banks also package the homes for sale to qualified investors. These investors buy REOs in bulk, and by picking up more than one home from the bank, they tend to receive better pricing.

However, no matter how you look at the sale of an REO property, the bank loses money. It is simply a matter of how *much* money the bank is going to lose.

Auction Foreclosure Stage

This is the second stage of foreclosure. When a home in foreclosure goes to auction, it means the home was advertised to sell on a certain day to the highest bidder on the courthouse steps. A public foreclosure auction is not to be confused with the types of auctions held by auction houses on behalf of sellers or lenders. Public auctions are generally held at the courthouse or in the lobby, but in some states, they are held at the property itself. The sheriff's representative, a trustee (normally on behalf of a title company), or other authorized representative posts the sale date of the property, and it is published in a newspaper of general circulation.

These homes are sold in *as is* condition, meaning there are no guarantees or warranties of the property's condition. Generally, they are sold for cash. The bank wants its money right then and there and often requests cashier's checks as payment in full. Investors show up and place cash bids. Sometimes there are many investors competing for the same properties, and sometimes nobody shows up at all.

It is complicated and dangerous to buy a foreclosure home at an auction, especially if an investor has never seen the home. Without a physical inspection, an investor may not know if the home has four standing walls or a roof, which makes buying foreclosures at an auction somewhat risky. Investors are urged to check out a home's condition before placing a bid at the auction. However, other circumstances could affect a home's marketability and profitability.

That risk depends on whether there are other liens filed against the property that take priority, because the investor is buying the bank's position in the property. If a junior lender is foreclosing, the first loan stays with the property. There might be tax liens, unpaid property taxes, mechanic's liens, or judgments in the public records, and all those liens will remain with the property.

Seasoned investors do their homework before bidding on a foreclosure at an auction. The novices do not make it past the first round, and the competition can be fierce. Most investors will not bid more than the bank's opening bid if they do not feel there is enough profit to realize in the home. If no one bids higher than the bank's bottom line, then the property is deeded to the bank, and that is how banks end up with REOs—because the mortgage balance is higher than the market value of the home, and nobody is foolish enough to pay over market value.

Pre-Foreclosure Stage

Before the home goes to public auction, it is in pre-foreclosure stage. State laws vary across the country, but generally, during the first few months of foreclosure, the owner has the right to make up the back payments and reinstate the loan, thereby calling off the foreclosure. Later in the foreclosure process, the owner must pay the loan in full to bring a stop to the foreclosure. A bankruptcy filing may also push off or delay the foreclosure.

Most owners in the pre-foreclosure stage would prefer to sell their home and try to protect their credit rating. I hate to say this, but the only way a credit rating will be protected is to sell the home at a high enough sales price to pay off the loans against the home. Owners with equity enjoy this option. Owners without equity, those whose loan balances exceed the value of the home, often lean toward the only remaining viable way to sell.

That choice is a short sale. Bear in mind that a short sale does not protect your credit rating, but it does offer its own advantages. You get peace of mind in knowing that you sold the home, and the bank did not get it. You also have the opportunity under Fannie Mae guidelines to rebuild your credit and qualify to buy another home in two years.

However, the secret to doing a short sale in the pre-foreclosure stage is to get the bank to accept a discounted payoff—that is to release the existing loan in return for a payment that is less than what is owed. Many banks, wanting to avoid the costly foreclosure process, will accept a short sale, but they are under no obligation to do so.

Home Equity Sales Act in California Applies to Pre-Foreclosures

If an owner occupant of a one- to four-unit dwelling is in the pre-foreclosure stage, certain California civil codes govern a pre-foreclosure sale if the buyer is an investor. Failure to comply with provisions of the civil code can result in a $25,000 fine, the buyer could serve up to a year in jail, and the seller will have the right to rescind the transaction for two years.

The Home Equity Sales Act was established to protect owners in foreclosure. Investor buyers must give the seller five days to cancel the transaction after the purchase offer has been signed, or until 8 AM on the day of the trustee's sale, whichever happens first. Investor buyers cannot accept delivery of any deed or instrument that conveys title to the buyer until this five-day period has passed. Moreover, real estate agents must provide proof that they are licensed to sell real estate in the state of California and a written statement to that effect. If real estate agents do not comply with this requirement, the agent and the buyer are liable for damages, and the seller may void the contract.

This means that if an investor buyer (a non-occupant buyer) approaches an owner in foreclosure, the investor and the investor's real estate agent must complete the appropriate documentation and give the owner five days to change his or her mind.

Under California law, prior to 2008, real estate agents were required to obtain a bond to represent an investor buyer, but a recent court ruling said that since a bond was unattainable, that restriction is unenforceable. Some of California's statutes, such as the bond requirement, made no sense from the beginning. While well intended, the bonds did not exist and could not be issued so that regulation made it impossible for a real estate investor to hire an agent to represent the investor. Fortunately, the California Appellate court in March of 2008 removed that requirement from the statute.

Foreclosure Rescue Fraud

Whenever people are in financial trouble, you will find shysters crawling out of the woodwork to offer assistance at the expense of another's misfortune. These types of companies and their employees prey on the naïve. They are wolves in sheep clothing. You can recognize them from their flashy Web sites and empty promises to help you. The truth is nobody, except a recognized and official nonprofit organization, will offer honest assistance.

Sellers want to believe these foreclosure scammers. After all, most people do not know anything about foreclosure or the foreclosure process. Most distressed sellers truly want to save their home. When they are offered an opportunity that sounds too good to be true, they want to jump on that offer.

They feel desperate. The scammers know this, and they take advantage of sellers in foreclosure. They might offer to pick up the back payments on the loan and stop the foreclosure in return for handing over a deed. Some promise the sellers that they can continue to live in the home and pay rent, but what often happens in these schemes is that the foreclosure rescue scammers never make any payments to the lender. Instead, they collect rent from the seller and put that money into their pockets.

Occasionally, you will run across a company that guarantees the seller can buy back the home after a certain period. They give false hope to those who are overwhelmed with urgency and anxiety. These companies find a hard-money lender to make a loan large enough to make up the back payments, and then they evict the sellers when they find another eager homebuyer to whom they sell the property.

When you sign over a deed to a foreclosure rescue scammer, you are giving away title and ownership of your home. You have no guarantee that the perpetrator will stop your foreclosure nor *ever* return ownership to you, regardless of the fraudulent paperwork handed to you. If you find yourself being hassled by one of these scammers and cannot afford a lawyer, contact your local Legal Aid Society for assistance or find a government agency to advise you.

Report foreclosure scammers to your local district attorney's office and the FBI. For more assistance, call the Homeowner's Hope Hotline at 1.888.955.HOPE or go to http://hopenow.com.

How to Avoid Foreclosure

The best way to avoid foreclosure is to prevent the filing of a Notice of Default. If you find that you are unable to make your mortgage payments, do not stick your head in the sand. Some homeowners feel apathetic, as though there is nothing they can do to save their home. Many become depressed. Some become so despondent that they take their own life in their hands.

In July of 2008, a woman from Tauton, Massachusetts, a quiet town about thirty-five miles outside of Boston, faxed a suicide letter to a lender hours before her home was scheduled for a public sale. Her letter predicted that she would be dead before the auction happened. None of her neighbors knew her home was in foreclosure. She had lived in that neighborhood for thirty-four years. Feeling hopeless, discouraged, and most likely embarrassed, this woman grabbed her husband's high-powered rifle and killed herself.

The news is full of tragic stories similar to this one. It is shocking and horrifying to imagine that people could be stressed over their financial affairs to the point that they see no way out but to end their own lives. I mention this not to frighten or offend anyone, but to say there are always options and alternatives and no need to believe falsely that you can do nothing. You can always do something.

If you cannot make your mortgage payment, the first step is to call your lender and ask for help. Do not make the mistake of throwing away mail from your mortgage company or stuffing unopened mail into a drawer. Your situation is not hopeless. Your mortgage lender might be agreeable to letting you work out a repayment plan that fits your budget and keeps you out of foreclosure.

In the best of all worlds, the mortgage lender might simply forgive one payment and let you begin making your regular payments in the following month. Although that rarely happens, it is worth asking the lender.

Sometimes, lenders will let you make up the missed payments by adding a little bit each month to your existing payments. For example, if your mortgage payment is $1,500 a month and you are two months behind, the lender might let you pay $1,700 a month for the next 15 months to bring your account current. This is an interest-free loan.

Another option is to modify the terms of your note. Maybe your interest rate is an adjustable rate, and you cannot afford to make the increased payment that results from a higher interest rate. Many of these types of adjustable-rate mortgages were originated five years ago, and times have changed. With the huge volume of foreclosure notices filed, many banks are deciding that an adjustable-rate mortgage is too volatile and are willing to lower the interest rate on those loans to keep them out of foreclosure.

If you are one of the lucky homeowners with equity, a lender might let you refinance your loan by adding the back payments into your mortgage balance, including the fees to refinance, and making you a new loan that is re-amortized for another thirty years. By increasing the term of your mortgage, you might find your payments are lowered and more affordable.

For homeowners with little or no equity, there is a Federal Housing Administration (FHA) refinance option, providing the existing lender will cooperate, and the owner qualifies. This reform was signed into law on July 30, 2008, by President Bush as part of the Housing and Economic Recovery Act of 2008. The program began on October 1, 2008.

This is a remarkable financing alternative for owners who are upside down, meaning they owe more than the home is worth. The refinance will place a new loan on the home at 90% of its appraised value—the market value of that home today, not the amount the owner paid for it.

To illustrate, say, you bought a home in 2006 for $300,000, but today that home is worth $200,000, yet you still owe $299,000. Under the new FHA refinance option, a lender would make a maximum loan of 90% of $200,000, which would result in a new loan of $180,000. This would drop your mortgage payment almost in half!

However, your existing mortgage lender would need to agree to accept a discounted payoff, less than what is presently owed. A lender might be agreeable to do this based on the comparable sales and to save money on having to foreclose. After all, if you stop making your mortgage payments, the lender will lose money. The lender will lose even more money if it ends up taking your home in foreclosure and then tries to sell it because the lender will not be able to sell that home for more than market value, which, in this case, is only $200,000. This means many lenders will agree to an FHA refinance, although the law does not force them to do it.

To qualify, owners must meet certain criteria. The first criterion is that the new monthly mortgage payment must not exceed 31% of the borrower's gross monthly income. Using the example above, a new mortgage payment based on a $180,000 loan, which includes taxes and insurance, might be around $1,500 a month. A borrower who earns $60,000 a year would have a gross monthly income of $5,000, which would be enough to qualify for this loan: $5,000 x 31% = $1,550 per month.

In effect, a homeowner would be trading a $299,000 loan balance for a loan balance of $180,000 and a much reduced mortgage payment. Sound too good to be true? Well, there is a catch. The catch is future appreciation—that is, any increase in equity at the time of sale—will be shared with FHA upon resale. The upside is many borrowers will be able to keep their homes, avoid foreclosure, and end up with an affordable loan. The downside is should a homeowner later sell, 50% to 100% of the future profits go to the government. That is the tradeoff. Nevertheless, it keeps a roof over the head of some families who could end up out on the street if they go through foreclosure.

The FHA refinance carries other restrictions. It is available only to those owners who occupy their residence. It is not available for investors or non-owner occupants. Homeowners must certify that they did not intentionally default on their loan nor commit mortgage fraud when they obtained their existing loan.

Unfortunately, because the FHA refinance is complex with rigid limitations, I believe that some homeowners who might qualify may not fully understand how the program works and, as a result, will dismiss the option. I imagine some people might blow a gasket and yell, "I'm not giving away any of *my* money to the government when I sell." I am confident some uninformed homeowners would rather lose their homes than participate in the FHA refinance program, and that is a shame. You may not hear about these folks, but they are out there, believe me. They are the type of people who enjoy throwing chairs around on *The Jerry Springer Show*.

2

Components of a Short Sale

Brief History of Short Sales

Short sales happen when a lender agrees to accept less than the amount that is owed by releasing the security for the mortgage and writing off the difference. This means if a homeowner owes, say, $300,000, but the home is worth only $200,000, the lender will lose $100,000 if it releases the loan. Some lenders would rather get part of their money than take the property in foreclosure.

During the housing recession of 1990–91, short sales were prevalent for a brief period. Then, they did not reappear until the summer of 2006. That is because real estate is cyclical. Sometimes, it goes up, and sometimes, it goes down. During housing booms, when properties are appreciating, people go wild and try to buy everything they can get their hands on, forgetting that values can decline. Overall, if you look at the big picture, you will see that the real estate market has continued to appreciate for the past fifty years, but that does not mean the market will be up when you need to sell.

Housing prices fell during World War I and stayed flat during the Great Depression and through World War II. Post war, prices began to spike. In the 1950s, modern construction methods allowed the mass production of homes, which helped to increase demand of real estate. Two gains in boom times of the 1970s and 1980s pushed values up again. After 1997, national housing prices climbed 83% to the end of summer 2006.

For people like me who were born in the 1950s, we have watched real estate values go up, dip a little, and go back up even further. For that reason, it is hard for some of us to fathom that real estate values could fall as dramatically as they decreased since 2006. Some real estate markets have experienced price drops of almost 50% between 2006 and 2008.

When property values fall, and a home is heavily leveraged, a homeowner can end up owing more than his or her property is worth. Leverage is the name of the game in real estate. It means you are using somebody else's money and not your own. Say you put down 10% and borrow 90% on a $100,000 home. If that home appreciates 10% over the next year, you just made $10,000 on your $10,000 down payment. That's a 100% return on your money.

Conversely, if you paid $100,000 cash for a home that rose 10% in value after one year to $110,000, you made 10% on your money. Likewise, if the value of that unencumbered home fell 10%, you lost 10% of your money. However, if you leveraged that purchase through a 90% mortgage, you lost 100% of your money. Leverage equals risk.

Homeowners who paid $100,000 in cash for a home that fell in value to $90,000 might be inclined to ride out the cycle and wait for the value to rise again. However, homeowners who financed 90% of their purchase and who owe $90,000 feel cheated. The mortgaged owners might say, "Why keep this house? It's not worth what I paid for it!"

Adjustable Rate Mortgages

In the late 1990s and early 2000s, many homeowners bought a home with no down payment whatsoever. They financed 100% of the purchase by using a combo mortgage, which is an 80% (of value) first mortgage and a 20% second mortgage. Buyers used a combo or piggyback mortgage for financing because it helped them to avoid paying private mortgage insurance (PMI), which is an extra premium lenders charge for a first mortgage that exceeds 80% of value. PMI insures the lender, so if the buyer defaults, the insurance company is on the hook for a deficiency.

Although a homeowner does need to fall behind on payments or wait for a notice of default to be filed before asking the lender to do a short sale, many lenders are more willing to cooperate when a homeowner is in foreclosure. It should not be that way; common sense says a lender would be smarter to keep its customer out of foreclosure than force the customer to go into foreclosure simply to negotiate the loan.

However, lenders are swamped with foreclosures. Many banks are understaffed and their employees are overworked. They cannot handle the volume of short sales and foreclosures in an expedient and efficient manner without hiring more employees. Banks that are already losing money generally are not willing to increase overhead to facilitate faster processing for short sales. It is almost as though they are treading water, trying to keep from drowning, and that is why many banks are throwing resources at the most dire circumstances that require immediate attention—those borrowers who are in default.

Hundreds of thousands of borrowers who took out an adjustable-rate mortgage or, even worse, an Option ARM, discovered the hard way that they could not make the increased mortgage payment when the interest rate adjusted. In the case of Option ARMs, many borrowers elected to make the minimum payment every month, which was less than interest. On those types of loans, interest accrued, and it was added to the principal balance of the loan, which resulted in a much larger loan than the original amount.

Some borrowers figured they would never be faced with making an increased mortgage payment because they believed that homes would continue to appreciate. They truly believed *that* day would never come. Perhaps their loan officer promised them they could refinance in a couple years when the property's value escalated or, in a worst-case scenario, they could sell. When home prices fell, those hopes vanished.

A small number of borrowers were simply naïve. They did not ask enough questions to understand the type of loan they were getting. Everybody else was jumping on the bandwagon to home ownership, so they hopped aboard, too. Lenders were processing so many loans that some did not stop to explain prepayment penalties, payment options, or the adjustment of the loan clearly.

Borrowers were told to sign the one hundred-plus mortgage documents placed in front of them, or they would not get the loan. Even if the borrowers tried to read the documents, the verbiage was filled with legalese terms and difficult to decipher. These borrowers later claimed that they were victims of unfair lending practices because they felt misled and deceived.

David bought a home in north Sacramento with an 80/20 combo loan. He paid a little over list price, too, to beat out competing offers. Shortly after he moved into the home, he decided he did not like the neighborhood. He complained to his agent that prostitutes hung out on the main drag a few blocks from his home, that his street had too much traffic; it appeared that some of his neighbors were dealing in drugs, and he could hear gunfire at night.

Nevertheless, when his roof began to leak, and he needed to make repairs, instead of selling the home, David decided to refinance his existing loan. Because properties were still appreciating six months after he closed escrow, David's home appraised for more than he paid for it. Therefore, he took out a much larger mortgage, paid for the needed repairs, and pocketed the rest of the cash.

By this time, David's mortgage payment was about $3,000 a month, and he continued to scrape up that money every month, even though it was a hardship on him. A year later, David decided it was time to sell. Except by then, his home was no longer worth what he paid for it, and his mortgage balance far exceeded the value of his home. He had to face the fact that either he would let his home go into foreclosure or he would stay. He chose to stay.

David was not a viable candidate for a short sale because he did not want to ruin his credit, and he could afford (although barely) to make his mortgage payments. A short sale for David might have also resulted in an unwanted penalty against him because he had refinanced his home. In California, all purchase money loans are exempt from deficiency judgments, but hard-money loans, such as a refinance, are not. To get a deficiency judgment, though, certain rules apply. This means David could have been held personally liable for the difference between what he owed the lender and the amount the lender received on a short sale if his lender had cared to pursue a judical foreclosure. If a deficiency judgment against him had been filed in the public records, David could never buy another property in Sacramento County without paying off that deficiency judgment.

Karen and Charles Buchanan (not their real names) were not as lucky. They owned a home in Land Park. Their mortgage broker was also licensed as a real estate agent but rarely sold any homes, which is not necessarily the best combination in this business. He talked the Buchanans into refinancing the home in Land Park and somehow obtained an appraisal for them at least twice as much as the home was worth. Then, they took that money and bought a home over the river in West Sacramento, thinking that they would easily sell the home in Land Park.

The mortgage broker had the home listed for about four months when the Buchanans called me to ask if I would list the home. We dropped the price in half and tried for a short sale. Even at that lower price, we received very few showings for a number of reasons. The home backed up to commercial property, it was located on a busy street, and it required a lot of work simply to bring it up to city building codes.

Vagrants broke in daily. It got to the point that when I showed it, I would stand on the steps and yell in my most authoritative voice: F-B-I. Sometimes I would hear footsteps scurrying out the back. Neighbors called me constantly to complain about the drunks sleeping in the bushes along the side of the house or about fronds flying off the palm trees and blocking the sidewalk.

I worked on selling this home for six months. Finally, we received an offer for the short sale. The Buchanans pulled together all the required documentation, we submitted the offer to the bank, and I continued to call the bank every day. The last communication I had with the bank was that even though the offer was less than its desired price, the bank was considering the offer and would postpone the trustee's sale. The following week, I received a phone call from an REO agent in another office. He told me the sale had been finalized, and he was wondering when he could get the key to sell it as a bank-owned property. The sellers and I were flabbergasted.

After this home was on the market for another six months as an REO, the bank finally sold it to an investor who paid $50,000 less than my short sale buyer had offered. The $550,000 mortgage was reduced to a final sales price of $190,000. This was crazy, and that was, for me, the first sign that the market for short sales made absolutely no sense. As time went on, it became more apparent to banks that they would lose money if they rejected a short sale, so they have been a bit more lenient. However, many banks had to learn the expensive lesson that this bank learned the hard way. I will tell you more about this transaction later.

Why Would a Bank Do a Short Sale?

When short sales first hit the market in a big way in 2006, many banks were reluctant to consider a short sale. Agents with less than fifteen years of experience, which is most of them, were unfamiliar with short sales. Some viewed a short sale as an opportunity to take advantage of the bank without realizing that bank managers, whose sole job is to assess the bank's bottom line carefully, run banks. I suspect these agents paid too much attention to the Get Rich Quick seminar schemes.

Banks are not in the real estate business—not yet, anyway. Several years had passed before bank managers figured out that the security for many of their loan portfolios had greatly diminished in value. In the beginning, banks relied on previous market value to establish comparable sales for their loans in default. If a home sold for $500,000 in 2005, it was inconceivable to imagine that that particular home might be worth $250,000 in 2007. Nevertheless, that is exactly what happened in many parts of the country.

In the beginning, banks were a pain in the butt. This next short sale in West Sacramento is a great example. The bank thought this home was worth about $350,000, but its true market value was closer to $225,000. I listed this home as a short sale and sixty days later received an offer, which I submitted to the bank. The offer was $220,000, and the bank initially rejected the offer. When I asked the negotiator why, she was rude, curt, and openly hostile to me. She explained that she ran the area comparable sales on her desktop, and the value she came up with was much higher.

As a rule, I am an easygoing, congenial person, or at least I like to think so. However, I can work myself into a lather if circumstances warrant, and this situation made it clear that I needed to communicate in a direct manner, using the same tone as the negotiator. I raised my voice slightly and spoke rapidly.

"The problem is you are pulling comparable sales for an area south of the subject property," I explained. "This home sits in a neighborhood about six blocks by six blocks square. It is the largest home in that subdivision, and it's missing a garage.

"One of the tenants was just released from prison, and from all appearances, he belongs to a gang. The other looks like a domestic abuse victim. They own a pit bull, live with five screaming kids, and refuse to let anybody into the house. They also haven't paid rent for three months. When evicted, they most likely will tear out the copper plumbing and trash the house if it's left standing at all.

"The buyer is willing to pay cash and buy this home as is, accepting responsibility for the tenants. If you don't want to short sale this property, then you can take it in foreclosure and end up selling it for $180,000 if you're lucky."

The negotiator promised to consider the offer. The following morning, she called to say the bank would accept the short sale.

I was ecstatic. I called the seller with the good news. However, the seller got greedy. He decided at that point that he wanted $1,000 for signing the paperwork. I explained that he was not entitled to receive any money from the sale of the home because sellers are not allowed to make a profit. He would not budge. He then suggested that I could give it to him out of my commission, under the table. We argued for twenty minutes, and it was clear that I might as well have been talking to my cat—except my cat would have licked my hand.

There was only thing one left to say to him, "Sir, I do not work with insane people, and you are insane." I canceled the listing. The property ultimately went into foreclosure, and the bank later sold it to a first-time homebuyer for about $180,000. Since the seller had previously refinanced the home, he had signed for a hard-money loan. The bank asked me why the seller refused to sign the offer, and I told the bank the truth—that he demanded cash under the table. The negotiator's response to me, "We are SO going after this guy." I imagine the bank did, too.

Banks typically take short sale offers to a committee. Everybody sits around the table and discusses the financial aspects and the effect on the bank's portfolio. They use comparable sales supplied to them by a real estate agent, alongside their own desktop appraisal, and sometimes ask an independent agent for a broker's price opinion (BPO). If the value of the home is close enough to the short sale offer, it often makes more financial sense for the bank to accept the short sale than to follow through to the completion of a foreclosure.

If the bank believes it can make more money by foreclosing, it will deny the short sale. However, other factors come into play as well. Banks will scrutinize the buyer's ability to close the escrow. Sometimes, they will ask to see the buyer's FICO scores or ask for a non-refundable deposit, and they always want to review the buyer's preapproval letter. If the buyer appears well qualified, and the price that is offered is somewhat reasonable, most banks will approve the short sale. They would be foolish not to.

When the short sale is approved, the bank makes specific demands. First, the bank will generally not pay for any repairs; the property is sold strictly "as is." The bank will negotiate the real estate commission and may pay the listing agent, conversely the selling agent, much less than the amount the seller agreed to pay.

Moreover, banks generally will not pay for inspections, home warranties nor any other fees considered unnecessary, which is why it is rare for a Veterans' Administration (VA) buyer to purchase a short sale since the VA has requirements for the buyer's loan that include completing pest work and other types of repairs. Buyers who obtain a conventional loan have a better chance at getting the bank to accept their short sale offers.

24

3

Short Sales versus Foreclosure Benefits

How Short Sales Affect Credit

A buyer's credit report plays an important role when buying a home. If a buyer has excellent credit and a high FICO score, the buyer will enjoy more favorable lending terms. Banks consider these types of buyers A-Paper clients, which means the interest rate offered will be lower, and the costs to obtain a mortgage will be somewhat reduced from standard fees.

The Fair Isaac Corporation created FICO scores. The corporation, established in 1956, was named for its founders, Bill Fair and Earl Isaac. Fair was an engineer, and Isaac was a mathematician. It is a complex credit-scoring system that produces a three-digit credit score. The higher the score, the better the credit rating. Scores range from 850 to 300, but few borrowers rank at the top end or the low end. A good credit score is considered 720. Borrowers can still obtain a decent loan with a score of 620. Below 620, the interest rates dramatically jump, and conventional lenders will not lend on those lower scores.

The FICO scoring system hit the big time in 1995 when Fannie Mae and Freddy Mac, the two mortgage giants that buy two out of every three mortgage loans, recognized the value in FICO scores and asked lenders to adopt this system. Nowadays, when a homeowner loses a property through the foreclosure process, the lender reports that foreclosure to the credit bureaus. This derogatory entry on a credit report causes FICO scores to plummet as much as 300 points or more. As a result, a person with a 720 FICO score could see that number drop to 420 or lower, which makes that person almost ineligible for any type of credit.

Moreover, mortgage applications contain a question that every borrower is expected to answer truthfully. It asks if a borrower has ever had a foreclosure within the past seven years. Borrowers who lie and check the "no" box when they have a loan foreclosed upon are subject to prosecution for mortgage fraud.

Catherine Coy is a mortgage broker from Huntington Beach, California. I asked her how a short sale affects credit versus a foreclosure. Was a short sale considered better? Did it mean the borrower suffered less of a FICO score loss by selling on a short sale? Ms. Coy responded, "The effect on a consumer's credit report, regarding a foreclosure vs. a short sale, is the difference between being hit by a train or a bus." In other words, both short sales and foreclosures affect a consumer's credit report the same, and it is a tragedy regardless of how you measure it.

Some homeowners are willing to take that hit to their credit report just to get rid of the house. They realize that over time they can rebuild and repair their credit report. In the credit-reporting world, the derogatory comment that shows up on a credit report is the entry Score Factor Code 22. The definition of Code 22 is *serious delinquency, derogatory public record, or collection filed.* Short sales and foreclosures fall under the latter. A short sale is not treated any differently than a foreclosure. They both result in the lender receiving less than the unpaid balance of the loan.

Fannie Mae and Freddie Mac require their lenders to report this type of derogatory credit to the three credit bureaus. This helps these institutions (now under government control) to assess correctly the risk posed by lending to future borrowers who have defaulted in the past or who have simply walked away from their financial obligations. Lenders use the borrower's past credit history to decide whether the borrower is a high- or low-risk candidate for a mortgage loan. They do not care if the borrower sold on a short sale versus a foreclosure. However, they take great care to avoid lending to a borrower with a Score Factor 22.

Under conventional guidelines, lenders want to see at least three credit lines that have been active for the past twelve months. Under guidelines that are more stringent for nontraditional loans, lenders expect to analyze a minimum of four accounts that have been in existence for at least twelve months. If they find a charge-off (short sale), a foreclosure, or a bankruptcy, that borrower will be considered a credit risk. The more recent the derogatory, the higher the credit risk.

Therefore, if a real estate agent tells you that the effect on your credit report is much less damaging for a short sale over a foreclosure, the agent is wrong. Think about this. If your home goes through the foreclosure process, the agent is not paid. If you do a short sale, the agent is paid. Some agents are misinformed, but some agents are motivated by a primary goal. They want to list your home, sell it to a short-sale buyer, and pocket the commission. That is the business they are in—listing and selling homes. I hate to say this, but although real estate agents are required to protect your interests beyond their own, some have set their sights on one purpose, and that purpose is to make a sale.

Not all real estate agents are created equal. They have different educational backgrounds and varying reasons for being in the business. Passing the same state exam to get a real estate license does not make one agent any more informed than another. It ensures they have the basic knowledge to pass the exam, but it does not make them an effective nor honest real estate agent. For this reason, it is imperative that consumers choose an agent who has integrity and whose performance is based upon ethics, not the dollar factor.

Having said all that, now I will contradict myself to say that there are a few cases where strong negotiation with a lender has resulted in no adverse credit, and the lender simply reported the short sale as "paid as agreed." However, those instances are rare.

How Soon Can You Buy Another Home after a Short Sale?

Because most short sales will affect sellers' credit ratings, no conventional lender that I work with will lend to a borrower immediately after a short sale. That does not mean, however, that if you have sold on a short sale, that you cannot immediately buy another home because you can. You just cannot finance it through a conventional lender. You will need to pay cash or obtain seller financing.

Now, this requirement could change in a few years after more short sales are cleared from the books, but for now, lenders are reluctant to set themselves up for another short sale because they view short sale sellers as high risk. They do not want to repeat the loss. Prior to August of 2008, lenders made no distinction between a short sale and foreclosure in terms of lending to those sellers a second time. The waiting period was a minimum of four years for Fannie Mae or Freddie Mac financing.

Fortunately, Fannie Mae set forth a new policy in the fall of 2008 that established a two-year period for reestablishing credit for short sales sellers. This new policy allowed buyers with a short sale on file to demonstrate that they have maintained an acceptable credit history since the completion date of the short sale and to qualify to buy again within two years. This was a huge and welcome change. It gave sellers in default a reason to try to sell on a short sale over a foreclosure.

Fannie Mae guidelines reset the seasoning period to buy again **after a foreclosure** to five years. It is easy to see why a seller might have an advantage for doing a short sale in lieu of a foreclosure now. Wait five years to buy or two years? It is not a difficult decision to make.

30

4

Waiting Period to Buy Again after a Foreclosure

Fannie Mae is less generous with its requirements for seasoning after a foreclosure. For example, the wait is five years to re-establish acceptable credit. However, it has other requirements, too, for post foreclosure sellers who want another mortgage. The home must be a principal residence. The buyer must put down a minimum of 10% of the sales price, and the borrower must show a minimum FICO of 680.

Extenuating Circumstances

For certain extenuating circumstances, Fannie Mae will knock two years off its seasoning guidelines for post foreclosure borrowers. Instead of waiting five years, a borrower can apply for a mortgage in three years, providing the borrower's credit is acceptable. However, bear in mind that the term *extenuating circumstances* means matters beyond a person's control.

Examples would be a death in the family that caused undo financial hardship, a job transfer or job loss, or a medical emergency such as an accident or sudden illness. It does not cover quitting a job nor divorce nor an inability to pay your mortgage because the interest rate increased. Extenuating circumstances do not apply to those who have decided that they can no longer afford to pay a mortgage payment due to a rate increase or a re-amortization feature of an Option ARM loan.

5

Buying a New Home before Defaulting on Your Existing Home

There are sellers who deliberately plan to let their home go into foreclosure but use their good credit to buy a new home before that happens. It is a scheme that does not work very well anymore and, in some instances, is against the law. Buying a new home before letting your existing home go into foreclosure is typically referred to as "Buy and Bail." This is how it works.

Say Susan owns a home in East Sacramento that is worth $400,000, but she owes $500,000 because she refinanced that home at the height of the home-buying frenzy in 2005. Because she is upside down on the home, Susan decides she no longer desires to continue paying on a mortgage, which will take her twenty-six years to pay off.

She also realizes that many homes in Sacramento are worth less than they were four years ago. Property values fell around 35% in Sacramento between 2007 and 2008. She has fallen in love with a home that she can buy for a song in the Arden Park neighborhood, and that home is much bigger than her existing home. Therefore, Susan decides to buy the home in Arden Park and let her East Sacramento home go into foreclosure *after* she closes escrow on the home in Arden Park.

Susan is smart enough to know that the lender will not make her a loan on the new home in Arden Park unless the lender believes that Susan will receive enough in rent to cover her mortgage payment on her existing home. Susan then asks a friend to sign a dummy rental agreement that shows her friend will rent the East Sacramento home for a bazillion dollars. She submits that rental agreement, along with her loan application and paperwork for the new home in Arden Park.

Just as soon as Susan's new loan is funded, and she receives title to the home in Arden Park, she stops making payments to the lender of her first mortgage. The lender for her East Sacramento home files a Notice of Default and initiates foreclosure proceedings. Susan does not care that her credit rating is trashed because she has already moved into her new home in Arden Park and does not plan to move again for a long time.

Some people might say, "What's wrong with that? That sounds like a good plan to me. Boy, is that Susan smart." However, what Susan has done is commit mortgage fraud. She lied on her loan application, and she submitted a phony rental agreement to the lender to get the loan. If her new lender had known what Susan was doing, that lender would not have approved Susan's new loan.

Lenders Are Cracking Down on Buy and Bail Schemes

Lenders are wising up. Now, if you want to turn your existing home into a rental, the lender will want to see a copy of your rental agreement and a copy of the rental check. You must have at least 25% to 30% equity in your existing home and may be required to qualify to hold both mortgages.

Knowing this, when a buyer called me to say he wanted to move out of his 2,000 square-foot home and buy a much smaller fixer REO property, I made the appointment to meet with him far enough in advance to give me ample time to check him out. I ran his name in the tax rolls to find his current address. Then, I pulled the comparable sales and compared those sales to his mortgage balance, which was also revealed in the tax rolls. Not surprisingly, he owed more than his home was worth.

I called him to share this information. "But my mortgage broker said I can do this," he complained. What could I say? His mortgage broker either lied to him or did not bother to run his desktop appraisal program to see that the home had no equity. He would not qualify, and I could not help him. Besides, a lender is not going to believe that a buyer will move into a 900-square-foot two-bedroom home in dire need of repair, even though some buyers with larger homes *would* trade—because it bucks the norm.

6

Taxes on a Short Sale

Talk about being kicked twice. As if it is not bad enough that a seller's home value may have dropped below the amount mortgaged, making a traditional sale or conventional refinance impossible, the IRS tax code allows for taxation on debt forgiveness.

It works like this. Say you have an outstanding mortgage balance of $200,000. When you bought your home, you paid $220,000 for it and put $20,000 down. However, comparable sales today show that your home is worth $150,000. Therefore, you find a buyer willing to pay $150,000. After months of negotiation with the bank, your mortgage lender agrees to take $150,000, less the costs of sale, and release the $200,000 loan. You walk away with no money in hand, but at least you are relieved that you can put this all behind you and get on with your life, right?

Not so fast. The lender may have the right to issue you a 1099-C for, say, $50,000, which is the difference between the amount you owed to the lender and the amount the lender received. (A tax basis is involved, but let's not quibble.) That is because you were relieved from having to pay $50,000, which is called debt forgiveness, and it is taxable as ordinary income. If you are in the 15% tax bracket, Uncle Sam could be there at tax time with his hand out, asking for $7,500.

Fortunately, the Mortgage Relief and Debt Forgiveness Act was enacted in December of 2007. This act allows sellers to exclude certain forgiven debt from taxation as long as the home was the seller's primary residence. It does not apply to investors. It pertains only to transactions that closed from 2007 through December 31, 2012 and includes canceled debt up to $2 million ($1 million if you are married and filing separately).

In some instances, a loan refinance will fall under the act, providing the funds were used to substantially improve, buy, or build your personal residence. If part of the canceled debt does not qualify for exclusion, it might under the following circumstances:

1) Insolvency. You are considered insolvent if your liabilities exceed your assets.
2) If the debt has been discharged under Title 11 of the U. S. Bankruptcy proceeding or if the debt is *qualified farm indebtedness* or *qualified real property business indebtedness*. See www.irs.gov for more information.

7

Short Sale Judgment Deficiency

I hate to throw another wrinkle into the mix, but sellers who are considering a short sale should find out whether the existing financing qualifies for a deficiency judgment because it may be possible that the lender can obtain a judgment for the difference between the amount it receives and the amount that was owed. It all depends on whether the loan qualifies and whether state law allows for personal liability regarding the mortgage.

California law excludes purchase money loans from deficiency judgments. This means the only security for a purchase money mortgage is the property itself. The lender cannot expect the owner to cough up the difference nor can the lender pursue a legal remedy to enforce it. A purchase money mortgage is a loan taken out to buy the home. It does not matter if it is a first mortgage or a home equity line-of-credit mortgage. As long as the funds were used to purchase the home, you are exempt from a deficiency judgment in the state of California.

However, refinances in California are not exempt. A refinance in California is considered a hard-money loan. A hard-money loan is a mortgage that was not used to purchase the home. These loans are either second or third mortgages, recorded against the home after the close of escrow, or they are a refinance of an existing loan. A refinance pays off the existing financing and puts new financing in place.

The problem with hard money loans in California is lenders have the right to pursue the borrower for a deficiency if certain guidelines are met. For example, if the first lender files a judicial foreclosure, that lender has the right to claim a deficiency. If the lender completes a trustee's sale, however, it cannot go back to the borrower for the deficiency.

Second loans are more complicated. Ordinarily, when the first lender files a notice of default, the second lender does not begin its own foreclosure proceedings because typically there is not enough equity to justify the expense. As a result, when the foreclosure is complete, the second lender's position is wiped out. If the second lender has lost the security for a hard-money loan due to foreclosure by the first lender, that lender, regardless of whether the foreclosure was judicial or by trustee's sale, has the right to pursue the borrower for the deficiency.

Borrowers in other states such as New York, for example, can sign loan documents that state they are personally liable for the loan. In the event of a default, the lender has the right to come after the borrower for a deficiency, providing the lender loses money either through a foreclosure or a short sale.

When a deficiency judgment is placed into the public records, it prevents a borrower from obtaining a loan to buy another home in that county. Because the deficiency judgment will take precedence, the new lender will require that it be paid off and a reconveyance recorded. A reconveyance is an official document that states the loan has been paid in full.

8

Property Qualifications for a Short Sale

Just because a property is listed for sale as a short sale, does not mean the property itself will qualify. For example, if the property is in bad condition and requires extensive repairs, a new buyer might face extreme difficulties getting a loan to buy it. The existing mortgage holder ordinarily will not pay for repairs or inspection reports. It will most likely insist that the property be sold in its *as is* condition.

More important, however, is the marketplace. If it is a seller's market, meaning it is a rising market with very little inventory for sale and many buyers, the lender might refuse to consider a short sale. The reason a bank would not approve a short sale under these conditions is that the bank might feel it can get a better price at the courthouse steps and get enough to pay off its loan.

If it is a buyer's market, meaning prices are falling and there is a lot of inventory for sale and very few buyers, the bank might think twice before deciding to reject a short sale offer. It might decide that it will lose money on a foreclosure and want to cut its losses before they get any worse. Moreover, if many homes in any given neighborhood are selling as short sales, the lender may feel it has no choice but to approve the short sale and write off a portion of its unpaid balance.

Before you decide to list your home as a short sale, ask your agent to tell you if it is a buyer's market, a seller's market, or a neutral market. Find out how many other homes in your immediate vicinity are for sale as a short sale, and find out how many of those have actually closed. You can use these numbers when you present an offer to the bank.

Types of Common Mortgages

Look at your loan documents, the papers that you signed when you took out your mortgage. Figure out your type of loan. Is it a conventional loan, an FHA loan, a VA loan, a subprime loan, or some other type of financing?

In California, some loans made to veterans are called CalVet. On a CalVet loan, the borrower does not have legal title because title does not transfer. Borrowers buy a home through CalVet on a land contract, meaning the title conveyed is only equitable title. CalVet loans are a bit more difficult to negotiate for a short sale. CalVet funds its loans by selling 30-year bonds.

CalVet makes 100% loans to qualified veterans, and its foreclosure rate is generally low. Although its interest rates are adjustable, they do not adjust more than ½%, which makes the loans very affordable for borrowers. By qualifying borrowers and limiting rate increases, CalVet is relatively assured that its borrowers will not default. However, should a borrower fall behind in payments, CalVet does have the right to initiate foreclosure proceedings.

The government insures FHA loans. That is why they carry mutual mortgage insurance (MMI), a portion of which is financed into the loan, and borrowers pay a small MMI payment every month with their mortgage payment. Conventional lenders fund FHA loans. If the lender faces a loss on the loan, the lender will look to FHA to pay some of its shortfall. Lenders might be more willing to negotiate a short sale when it will recoup part of its loss through FHA.

Prior to January 1, 2009, FHA borrowers were required to put down a minimum of 2.85% of the purchase price. After that date, the minimum down payment requirement for FHA changed to 3.5%. Why the government wants to make it harder for buyers to come up with a down payment in a depressed economy is beyond me, but most likely, it has a political reason for it. If an FHA loan goes through to foreclosure, then the lender makes a claim to the insurance company for that portion covered by insurance. However, the property most likely reverts to HUD, Housing and Urban Development.

VA loans are made to veterans. They require no down payment. Veterans must qualify by having good credit, an acceptable employment history, and a certificate of eligibility from the VA. The Veterans Administration guarantees the loan, which a conventional lender funds. If the borrower defaults on the loan, the VA pays the lender's claim and takes back the property.

As with FHA loans, lenders can make a claim for part of their losses during a short sale, so VA loans are also likely candidates for a short sale. Dan Tharp, CMPS (Certified Mortgage Planning Specialist) at Vitek Mortgage Group in Sacramento, says he understands that both VA and FHA will cover part of the losses for short sale transactions, but exactly how much can vary.

Conventional loans are those funded by traditional lenders and may or may not be packaged and sold in the secondary market. The conforming loan limit is $417,000. (Each bank makes up its own rules for short sales, and no two banks handle short sales in the exact same manner, which can make the process complicated and even frustrating at times. You would think banks would somehow get together and decide on a uniform format for short sales, but that will happen when pigs can fly.)

Conventional loans can be adjustable-rate mortgages, fixed-rate mortgages, interest-only mortgages, or a combination of all three. Some of the major players in the conventional market are Bank of America, Wells Fargo, and Washington Mutual. (The U.S. federal government seized Washington Mutual in September of 2008, and JPMorgan Chase acquired the assets.)

Conventional loans can also be the most difficult, primarily because conventional lenders' policies can change from one day to the next, and because they are understaffed. It is common for a lone negotiator to handle 500 or more files a month. Sometimes, one department does not know what another department is doing, which makes effective communication challenging.

Subprime loans are those made to borrowers who do not qualify for a preferred rate conventional loan, because the borrowers' FICO scores were too low. Typically, these loans are adjustable-rate mortgages. They might carry an Option ARM feature, which essentially lets the borrower pick a payment such as amortized, interest-only, or even less than interest-only. If a borrower chooses a less-than-interest payment, the unpaid interest is added to the loan balance, which increases the loan balance. This is known as negative amortization. The interest charged for these loans is generally much higher than rates given to preferred borrowers. The loans contain prepayment penalties, making it impossible, in some cases, to refinance.

Some borrowers who took out subprime loans were not really qualified in the first place to obtain financing. The borrowers might have received what is called "a liar loan," or more commonly called "stated income, no doc." This means the borrower did not produce bank statements or a list of assets for the bank to verify. The borrower *stated* income (made up a salary), and employment was not verified. In some cases, loans were made to individuals who did not have a job. If they were employed, they might have been gardeners, for example, or hamburger flippers, earning minimum wage, but their loan applications might reflect a much higher income.

While the subprime mortgage market is not completely responsible for the rise in foreclosures, it certainly plays a prominent role. A logical person might ask how or why these loans were ever made in the first place, but the fact is if a borrower with somewhat decent credit in 2005 could fog a mirror, that borrower could get a loan, and many subprime loans were made to unqualified individuals.

Banks with a high volume of subprime loans in their portfolios were the first to fold and go into receivership. More will fail as the foreclosure shakeout continues. As a result, many subprime lenders are eager to get rid of these loans, and they will bend over backward to work with a short sale buyer.

9

Comparative Market Analysis

The common thread that runs through the process for all these loans is every bank will want to establish the value of a property before assessing a short sale offer. There are many ways to establish value, but the three most common ways are by a Broker Price Opinion (BPO), a Desktop Appraisal, or a Comparative Market Analysis (CMA).

A BPO is a mini appraisal done by an independent real estate agent, and the bank might pay the agent's broker a small fee for services rendered. Critics' objections to a BPO are sometimes the agent is not familiar with the neighborhood and may include comparable sales that do not lie within the boundaries of that specific neighborhood. The agent might do a *drive by* and not personally inspect the property to determine its condition.

A desktop appraisal is, of the three, the least likely to produce an accurate determination of value. This procedure is typically a computer-generated appraisal. Again, no one specifically inspects the property. The software selects properties within a certain radius of the home. If a true radius is used, that may constitute a circle around the existing home, and by its circular and not square nature, except certain sold homes from the computation.

Comprehensive CMAs will include extensive information. First, boundaries are set according to the neighborhood dynamics. Some areas are identified by geographical boundaries such as bordering a railroad line or a major intersection. Homes that are located on either side of these boundaries may vary greatly in value, depending on the neighborhood. This is where a neighborhood specialist can be of great value to help determine value.

Next, similar types of properties are compared to each other and adjusted for certain features. Unbelievably, one can apply a dollar figure to square footage variances. An extra bedroom, for example, has a definitive value. Generally, the closer the features match the subject property in both size, age, and configuration, the more accurate the CMA.

Active listings are used only for informational purposes but not necessarily for value. That is because a seller can ask any price a seller wants for a piece of property. I could ask $3 million for my home, but if it is only worth half a million, the listing price means nothing. However, if a large percentage of the homes in a particular neighborhood are for sale as short sales or foreclosures, those sale-price values might be lower than the comparable sales, which then makes those listings important to the CMA.

Pending sales—those homes that have a contract accepted but have not yet closed—tell a story, too. Especially, if one can find out how much they sold for by calling the listing agent. Pending sales will turn into hard comparable (sold) sales, typically during the term of contract on the short sale. They predict which way the market is moving. However, it is not always possible to find out the sales prices until they actually close.

The sold homes carry the most weight, particularly those

that have sold within the last three months. That is because those homes are the basis for reflecting what a willing buyer paid and the price at which a willing seller sold. Homes that are similar in size, configuration, age, and condition and close to the subject property will be used to establish market value.

Withdrawn, expired, or canceled listings show that there was something wrong with those properties, and that problem is generally price. They were priced too high for the market. If the bank claims a value for the home that is close to those expired listings, the argument can be made that the home will meet the same fate as those that did not sell. The median sales price of expired or canceled listings is typically much higher than the median price of the active listings.

Location plays the most important role. In the case of the duplex in Land Park that the bank rejected, no matter how many ways I explained it, the bank refused to believe that the home was located in a bad location. It kept comparing the home to others in Land Park that were in desirable locations. This particular property backed up to a gas station; it was a block from a major cross street in Land Park; and it sat on the corner of a busy street. The bus stop was a half block away, and homeless people slept on the bus bench and in the bushes alongside the home. The only way to get a location worse than this was to put the home in the middle of the city dump.

Fortunately, most banks understand a CMA, and they will put more faith in the agent who knows the neighborhood, the home's inherent characteristic value, and who has personally inspected the home. You must prove to the bank why the home is worth the short sale offer; otherwise, the bank has limited information on which to base an opinion and will ultimately reject the short sale offer.

10

Seller Qualifications for a Short Sale

Not only must the property qualify for the short sale, but the seller must qualify as well. The primary reason is if the lender is going to take a loss, the lender most likely will not agree to the short sale if the seller has enough assets or cash on hand to pay the short fall. In other words, it is almost impossible to ask the lender to take the hit if you are capable of paying the lender yourself.

This does not mean you cannot have assets such as stocks, bonds, retirement funds, cash, or a well paying job, as long as the total amount of your liabilities match or exceed your assets. Most short sale sellers do not have the problem of too many assets. Some are unemployed, and that is the best type of seller to be. If you have no income, it is easy to prove a hardship to the lender.

Lenders will ask for a hardship letter. The more pathetic a seller can make it sound, the better. The beginning of the letter should explain how you got into this situation. Good reasons are being laid off; getting a divorce; dealing with an illness in the family or your own medical emergency; or having financial difficulties such as identity theft, excess credit card debt, a gambling addiction, or having to pay off a judgment from a lawsuit. Those are sound and legitimate reasons.

You should write the letter, preferably in your handwriting, and it should read as though it comes from the heart. Tell the story in excruciating detail. Describe how you tried to remedy the situation to no avail. Make your situation sound hopeless. Realize that the bank will understand that it cannot squeeze money out of a beet. You really want to show that you are at the end of your rope, and selling your home on a short sale is the only way out. Do not let the bank believe you have other options. Prove that you have exhausted all your resources, and be truthful.

Rental Properties

As discussed earlier, you will not avoid paying taxes on the debt forgiveness if you are an investor. Only owner occupants can exclude debt forgiveness from income for tax purposes. However, rental properties do qualify for a short sale if they are upside down, meaning you owe more than the rental's market value. If you are hoping to sell a rental property on a short sale, the best thing you can do is evict the tenant before putting the home up for sale.

It is understandable that some rental property owners are reluctant to tell the tenant to move out. After all, the tenants most likely are paying rent. If your mortgage is going into default, that rent money could be going into your bank account, and it is extra income to you. In states where the security instrument for the mortgage is a deed of trust with *assignment of rents*, the lender has the right to step in and collect the rent from your tenant. Some lenders do not go to that trouble, but some do. Why would you want to let your tenant pay the lender instead of you?

When you prepare a balance sheet for the lender, that rent would show as income to you, and it might disqualify you in the lender's eyes from a hardship. Another reason to get rid of the tenant is tenants make it hard to show the property. Most states have laws that require at least 24-hours' notice before showing a property, and tenants are likely to know their rights. Many tenants will not let an agent put a lockbox on the property to provide access to other agents, and that will hamper the showings.

Look at this way, if there are many upside down homes on the market, agents are going to show those that provide easy access. Agents often do not have the time to make an appointment or call 24 hours in advance. Even if they do manage to call, some tenants will not cooperate and will come up with lame excuses as to why the agent cannot show the home. And why should tenants show the home? There is nothing in it for them. It is an inconvenience for them.

Tenants rarely keep the home in spic and span condition around the clock. They do not want to be bothered to clean up the house or leave when agents show up with buyers. I cannot count the number of tenant-occupied homes I have shown that have been filthy—dirty dishes in the sink, cigarette butts in ashtrays, clothing strewn about the floor, unmade beds. A home needs to sparkle to attract a buyer's attention, and tenants are unlikely to accommodate your wishes.

You want to let agents show your home when it is convenient for the agents to show it. Ideally, this means the home should be vacant, and a lockbox should be located on the premises. Otherwise, agents will show other homes, and buyers will never see your home.

If those are not enough reasons to convince you that it is a good idea to show the home empty, think about this. Some states require that tenants be given a specific number of days to move. If you wait until the home goes under contract, and the bank accepts the short sale offer, there might not be enough time left before the close of escrow to give the tenant enough time to move out. The buyer for your rental will most likely be a first-time homebuyer, and first-time homebuyers do not want to wait another 30 or 60 days to move into their first home. They want to move in when it closes. If they cannot, they will buy another home that *is* available for occupancy at closing.

Moving the Tenant

Sometimes, tenants are very cooperative, though, and they will surprise you. A very nice man, I will call him Jeffrey, was a tenant of a short-sale client. The process began in September, and by May, we had begun to make progress with the bank. This was a horse property, almost three acres in Rio Linda, a city just north of Sacramento. My client had bought this home for $700,000 two years prior. Now it was worth about $400,000.

The buyer was willing to wait the eight months for an answer from the bank because she owned horses, and there were not very many properties for sale at that price. This was the perfect home for her.

Jeffrey set appointments with a huge number of buyers and their agents to see the home. He was unaware that the home was in default and trusted his landlord to take care of him. When the bank finally approved the short sale, it wanted to close within two weeks. The buyer was ready to close by that time as well. The problem was how to relocate the tenant. He had rights. He should have received notice to vacate the premises months earlier, but the seller did not want to lose the rental income.

The seller was in a pickle, and by extension, so was the buyer. I suggested that the seller pay the tenant to move, but the seller did not have any extra cash lying around. I crossed my fingers and called the tenant. "Jeffrey, this home is in foreclosure. The bank has sold the property, and the new buyer is moving in at the end of the month." I thought being honest was the best way to approach this. I apologized profusely. I thanked him for all of his assistance for showing the property. Jeffrey promised to try to find a new home.

A week later, Jeffrey called to say he had been unsuccessful. He needed a particular configuration and a certain price, and there were not any rentals available at that price in Rio Linda or in nearby Citrus Heights. Then it dawned on me. I could ask my fellow real estate agents if they had clients who own rental property in those areas. I found an agent whose client lived out of town. She indeed did have such a property, and it was vacant. Eureka! The only problem was the rental amount was too high. Therefore, I asked the agent if her seller might consider a reduced rental amount for a long-term tenant with great references.

She agreed to knock $200 a month off the rent. Jeffrey got his place, and he moved that weekend. Whew! Talk about being down to the wire. If Jeffrey had wanted to, he could have refused to move. His landlord did not give him legal notice. Sometimes you just get lucky, but it is rare. If you have a choice, please give your tenants the required notice to move and put your home on the market when it is vacant. You will save yourself a ton of headaches down the road.

Preparing Your Net Worth Statement

In addition to your hardship letter, the bank will want to see your financial statement. It does not have to be submitted on a form, but it should contain a list of all your assets and all your liabilities.

Start with cash in the bank. Make a list of every bank account, all checking, savings, money market, and CDs that you own, and itemize the cash on hand in each. For many people, this will be easy. You might have $200 in a checking account and $25 in savings. For others, it will be more complicated.

Next, compile a list of your retirement accounts and stocks/bonds, if any. Look at your most recent statement from the financial institution to figure out today's value. This is not the cost of those investments, but rather, what are they worth on the day you fill out your financial statement. If you do not know the value, you can go online to finance.yahoo.com and find the value by entering the mutual fund or stock symbol.

Your automobiles have a value as well. Go to Kelley Blue Book online at http://kbb.com. Search by year, make, and model. Then, enter specifics such as upgrades and miles. This Web site will give you an approximate value of each vehicle. Do not worry about how much you owe to the bank on an automobile loan because that comes later. For right now, the only thing you need to be concerned about is your car's market value.

It is unlikely for most people, but if you have debtors who owe you money, that, too, is considered an asset and would need to be listed.

If you own other real estate, list the market value of each property. You can get an approximate number by going to Zillow.com and entering the property address. It is not a perfect system, and sometimes Zillow is way off on value, but if your real estate is located in a conforming area where most of the homes look identical to each other, it might be a very close value. You might also call a local real estate agent and ask for a list of comparable sales to determine value yourself. At this point, do not concern yourself with any mortgage secured to other property. Just find the value.

Your household furniture and your personal belongings, including clothing, have a value. It is probably nowhere near what you paid for it. You would be safe if you figured a value based on 15% to 25% of the amount it initially cost. If you are confused because, say, you just bought a big screen Sony TV, go to Craigslist.org or eBay.com. Search for that Sony TV to see the prices advertised for used TVs.

Pull out your insurance policies, and read them. If they have a cash value if you surrendered the policy, that amount is considered an asset. If you have a term-life insurance policy that stipulates the policy is canceled if you stop making payments, it does not have a cash value.

List other valuables such as jewelry, guns, artwork, coin collections, and antiques, and determine the value of each. Typically, these types of valuables are noted on a rider to your insurance policy and appraised for that purpose. If you have an appraisal, use it.

Total the value of all your assets, and enter that total at the bottom of your list of assets. You might be amazed to discover you are worth that much but do not yet despair, because some of those assets will be encumbered and the total value will be reduced when offset by your liabilities.

Figuring your assets is probably the most difficult part of a financial statement. Next, let's look at your liabilities. This section will include everything that is a debt to you.

You want to do two things when figuring out your liabilities: list the total amount that is due, and on a separate sheet of paper, list the monthly payments you make. This way, you will create a list of total liabilities on one sheet and, on the other, a list of total monthly payments.

If you are making payments without security for the debt to an individual and have signed a promissory note, that is most likely an unsecured note and a liability. For example, say your parents loaned money to you to buy a car or make a down payment on a house. Find the agreement between you and your parents, and include that amount on your list of liabilities.

A promissory note generally secures mortgages, and the financing document is recorded in the public records. The financing document can be a deed of trust or a mortgage, depending on your state laws. If you are in default, your mortgage company will have sent you an itemized statement that shows the unpaid balance and all amounts due to bring the mortgage current. You can use that unpaid total.

If you are not yet in default, look at your last mortgage statement, which will reflect the unpaid balance, and use that number. Although your balance will drop after making a payment, it will not go down enough to really matter on your bottom line. That is because payments are credited first to interest and second to principal. The principal reduction is insignificant to the overall picture.

All unpaid property taxes are a lien against the property and a liability to you. Depending on how your tax year is configured, it may be difficult to figure which taxes are unpaid and what the amount due is. You can start by looking at an old tax statement. It will show you the period the taxes cover and how much you have paid. Many tax assessor offices are online, too.

Even if your taxes are not yet due, they may constitute a liability. You can figure out the amount of months that are not yet paid and add that to your liabilities. For example, taxes in California cover the period from July 1 to June 30. They are paid twice a year. The first half (July 1 to December 31) is due by December 10. The second half (January 1 to June 30) is due by April 10. If today is March 31, a Californian already owes three months of taxes. To figure out the dollar amount, divide your annual taxes by twelve months and take that number times three.

Any unpaid taxes that you owe to the state government or to the federal government (IRS) are also a liability. If you have not yet paid your taxes for the previous filing year, you can include those sums. For example, if today is March 31, 2009, and you owe taxes for the calendar year of 2007, you can include that sum plus penalties to date. If you have not filed your return for 2008 (because it is not due until April 15, 2009) or because you have filed for an extension and cannot afford to pay those taxes, you can include your tax liability for 2008 on your financial statement.

If it is of any condolence to you, I would rather poke my eyes out with a hot poker than compute my taxes, which is why I have an accountant. If you do not have an accountant or cannot afford to pay a tax expert, you can use a tax computing software program such as Turbo Tax to come up with an estimate for your present year's tax bill.

How much do you owe on your car? Is it paid for, or are you making payments to the dealer or the bank? Find your last statement, which will reflect your unpaid principal balance. You can also call the entity to which you make payments and ask how much you presently owe. Add that amount to your list of liabilities. List your car payment separately on the monthly budget sheet under liabilities.

The biggest headache for many people is the process of sorting through credit card statements. If you pay your bills online, you may need to go to each creditor's Web site, and that could entail remembering a bunch of user names and passwords. Otherwise, if you have a paper trail, pull out each credit card statement and write down the name of the creditor and your unpaid balance. List the total of your monthly credit card payments separately on the monthly budget sheet under liabilities.

Sometimes, people will keep making the minimum payment due on credit cards but forego making payments to the doctor, dentist, or hospital. If you have outstanding medical bills, list those as well. Put the total outstanding balance on the liabilities sheet and the amount of payments you make on the monthly budget sheet under liabilities.

Call your insurance agent, and ask that person to FAX or e-mail you a list of upcoming insurance notices that contain the amount of each insurance premium. This would include payments toward a life insurance policy, the amount due for your automobile insurance, flood insurance (if any), and your homeowner's insurance. Total your insurance premiums, and divide by 12 to get your monthly estimated insurance payments. List your insurance premiums on the monthly budget sheet under liabilities.

If you do not save your grocery receipts, look to the method by which you buy groceries. If you charge them, the amounts will be noted on your credit card statements. If you pay cash, figure out approximately how much you take out of the bank to cover your grocery bill every month. If you pay by check, look in your check register. Total the last three months' of grocery receipts, and divide that number by three to get an average amount you spend each month on groceries. List that bill on the monthly budget sheet under liabilities.

Think about other ways you spend money in any given month. How much do you pay for home repairs, dry cleaning, gas for your car, oil changes/service for your car, childcare, clothing, medical, telephone, gas/electricity/water for your home? Add those amounts to your monthly budget sheet under liabilities. Do not add entertainment options such as the cost of movie or concert tickets, eating out, club memberships, cell phones (unless used for business), or family vacations.

Now, the fun begins. Add up the total unpaid balances of your liabilities, and subtract that total from your total assets. If your asset number exceeds your liability number, you have a positive net worth. If your liability number exceeds your asset number, you have a negative net worth. The closer you can come to having a negative net worth, the better you will appear as a candidate for a short sale.

Next, take your net monthly income, and subtract the payments you make every month. If you have money left over, you have a positive cash flow. If you spend more than you take home, you have a negative cash flow. Remember, the closer you are to a negative cash flow, the better you will appear as a candidate for a short sale.

Do not be surprised if you take home less than you pay out. Many families do. It is almost the American Way. Now might be a good time to examine closely where you spend money every month and decide whether you can improve this budget in the future, by either cutting back on expenses or increasing your income. It is sort of like going on a diet. There is only one way to lose weight—eat less and exercise more. The same principle applies to a personal budget—earn more and spend less.

Keep the asset and liability sheet and your monthly budget sheet to submit to the lender.

11

What Paperwork Lenders Require for a Short Sale

As a mortgage broker friend of mine says, sometimes lenders can make demands for paperwork, and it is not possible to provide it. She says one borrower told her, "I ain't got no job, no money, and no bank account, so I can't give you nuthin." I am not suggesting that you apply that approach to your situation, even if it is remotely similar. Refusing to cooperate just makes it all that much harder to get your short sale accepted.

Some listing agents prefer to assemble the documents for their short-sale sellers in a three-ring binder, neatly compiled with tabs that identify the contents. Does not matter. The bank is likely to lose your paperwork anyway. So, be smart and make copies. You can FAX the documentation to the bank, but I also suggest sending a package in overnight mail, with signature required for delivery. The person who signed for your package might still be working at the bank a few weeks later, and you can track down that individual, but do not count on it.

Following is a list of the most commonly requested items. Some banks ask for additional documents, and some want less paperwork. It is better to be prepared in advance. Do not submit any paperwork to the bank until you have received an offer, because until you have a willing and able buyer, the bank will not care.

The hardship letter.

This is your sad tale of woe, told in your personal voice and style. As we discussed earlier, you want to tell the story of how you got into this situation, what you have done to get out of it, and where you stand today. If you have a particularly unusual incident to report such as you shot and killed a man in Reno, include it, but remember to be truthful.

Representative letter of authorization.

The bank will not discuss your mortgage with anyone other than you, unless you give the bank written authorization to do so. It does not need to be complicated. You can say that you authorize the bank to discuss your mortgage with NAME OF PERSON. Date the letter, include your loan number, your name, the property address, and your real estate agent's name and contact information. Then, sign it.

To download a free sample representative letter of authorization, go to TheShortSaleSavior.com and sign up for the free Short Sale Savior report. You will receive a link to your free documentation kit that includes sample letters.

When you give the letter to your agent, also give the agent the last four digits of the primary borrower's social security number—not the entire social security number. Many banks request this information as a security measure when talking to your agent by telephone.

Listing agreement.

The bank will be interested in reviewing the listing agreement. If you have made several price reductions over the course of the listing agreement, include those modifications as well. It will show the bank that you tried to sell your home at a higher price, but the market was not biting. The listing agreement also indicates how long ago the home had been listed.

Purchase contract.

We can only hope that the selling agent has crossed all the t's and dotted all the i's correctly. Because banks so rarely consider paying for certain items, make sure, if you can help it, that your contract does not include such seller-paid requests as home warranty plans, pest inspections and clearance, buyer's closing costs or down payment credits, buyer rebates or concessions, and, especially, not any fees that a seller does not customarily pay for in your county. For example, if the seller does not customarily pay for the buyer's owner's title insurance policy, do not ask for it.

If you have to ask the buyer's agent to rewrite the offer or change the terms on an addendum, then do it. You want to submit a clean offer. The offer should include a photocopy of the earnest money deposit. I am not saying that banks never pay certain requested fees, but the odds are not in your favor of it happening.

Short sale addendum.

Some states use a short sale addendum (SSA) that is made part of the purchase contract. The California Association of Realtors (C.A.R.) has published a C.A.R. form SSA for this purpose. The SSA specifies that the purchase contract is contingent on the lender's approval and lets the buyer indicate the date by which the approval should be received. If the lender does not approve the purchase contract by that specific date, the buyers have the right to cancel the purchase contract.

Other important aspects allow the inspection period to begin the day after the buyer receives the short-sale lender's consent and the buyer's earnest money deposit to be held uncashed until the lender approves the transaction, providing the appropriate boxes are checked.

Preliminary title report or title commitment.

If you have obtained a copy of the preliminary title report—in some states, it is called a title commitment—submit that with your paperwork. It will show who is presently in title, the liens recorded against the property, the amount of unpaid taxes, and the legal description, among exceptions to coverage.

W-2s, income tax returns, and pay stubs.

Make copies of your tax returns and W-2s for the past two years. Do not enclose originals. Check to make sure your tax returns are signed. If you filed electronically, your copies may not be signed. Include copies of your last two pay stubs.

Bank statements.

Pull the last three months of bank statements from every financial institution. Carefully examine the deposits. If you have deposited money into an account above and beyond a payroll check, you may need to include an explanation. The bank will want to know why you are receiving income and from whom. Attach a separate letter that explains additional or unaccounted for deposits.

Financial statement.

This is the list of assets and liabilities that you have previously prepared. It should reflect your monthly in-flow and out-flow of cash, including the total amount of assets owned by you and the total number of your liabilities. By subtracting the liabilities from your assets, you will arrive at your net worth. By subtracting your net monthly income from your monthly expenses, you will arrive at the cash flow left over every month, if there is any.

Comparative market analysis or appraisal.

The least expensive way to obtain this information is to ask your real estate agent to prepare a CMA for you. You have the option and the right to pay for an independent appraisal, but it will cost you, and you might not obtain the value you desire. The most weight will be given to comparable sales that have sold within the past thirty days to three months. This will establish the basis for your negotiation with the lender and is an important reason why the lender should accept the purchase offer.

It is entirely possible that the bank will not require every document listed above. The bank might also ask for other documents not mentioned. Every bank is different, and each operates by its own procedures. As a safety precaution, make sure you make copies of everything you send to the bank because, as I mentioned earlier, banks have a way of losing or misplacing the paperwork. After you have gone through all this work to compile the information, you most likely do not want to repeat the process.

12

Working with a Short-Sale Real Estate Agent

Reasons to Hire an Agent

Experience.

Ask if the agent specializes in short sales. If the agent you have in mind has never done a short sale, that person is not a viable candidate, regardless of how much you may like or trust the agent. Experience means the agent has negotiated with a variety of lenders and may possess specific knowledge about your lender. Experience also means the agent should have learned from past mistakes and will not make those mistakes again.

Degree of separation.

You really do not want to deal directly with buyers who are hoping to steal your home. Buyers who pursue a short sale primarily do so because they hope to get a good deal. By hiring an agent, you are removing yourself from direct involvement with the buyers.

Familiar with neighborhood sales.

Most homeowners hear about new listings when they come on the market but often do not know for how much the homes sold. Unless you have been inside each of your neighbor's homes, you also do not know the condition of those homes or whether they had significant improvements, both of which affect value. By hiring a neighborhood specialist, you can be relatively assured that the price the agent suggests to you is the price at which your home will sell.

You do not pay the agent.

Even though you will be asked to sign a listing agreement, the lender will pay the agent's commission. You will pay nothing. The fee to the listing agent is paid from the sales price, along with the other costs of sale, which a seller under ordinary circumstances would pay, but a short-sale seller does not.

Marketing and advertising.

The listing agent will absorb the cost to market and advertise your home for sale. This may include printing flyers and sending direct mail postcards. Your home will be listed on a multiple listing service, which other real estate buyer's agents can access. Agents have marketing systems in place, which can streamline the process for them at an efficiency rate most sellers cannot begin to duplicate by themselves.

Trend data.

To help support your claim for a lower sales price, your real estate agent can gather data from the last year to show neighborhood trends. This may include monthly totals of average sales price to list price, the number of days on market, the amount of homes for sale versus the number sold, and the number of months it will take to absorb the entire inventory presently available for sale.

Networking.

Many real estate agents maintain membership in the National Association of Realtors and, by extension, their state and local boards of realtors. Local boards hold meetings where agents network and promote listings. Agents who have been in the business for a while will maintain established relationships with other agents who also work in the same neighborhoods. This exposure to other agents will help to sell your listing faster.

Negotiation.

Short-sale agents have the knowledge and expertise to negotiate with the loss mitigator or negotiator at the bank. They are known for not taking "no" for an answer and will diligently work toward reaching a mutually acceptable agreement from the bank. Professional negotiation skills go beyond asking if the bank will accept an offer. They entail showing the bank why it is in the bank's best interest to take the offer on the table.

Paperwork submission.

A short-sale specialist will assemble and submit all the paperwork to the bank for you and make copies just in case the bank misplaces your file. Agents know what the bank wants in the file, so there is very little second-guessing or trying to find a document at the last minute.

Fiduciary responsibility.

Because your agent will represent you and not the bank, the agent will be required to hold your interests above those of the agent. It means your agent must keep all your personal and financial information confidential and not disclose any private facts that you have not authorized to the bank or any other party to the transaction. The agent must be loyal to you and disclose all material facts to you. The agent cannot share any of your confidential information to the buyer.

Customer satisfaction.

The bank is not going to care if you are happy when the transaction closes. In fact, the bank does not care if you are happy right now. You have no leverage with the bank. However, your real estate agent cares, if for no other reason than the fact that happy clients refer other business. Most real estate agents build their business on client referrals. If you are satisfied with the service and guidance your agent provided, then you will tell your friends, family, and coworkers about this agent. The agent has an additional incentive to ensure customer satisfaction.

How to Find a Short-Sale Agent

Many sellers who are headed into default may prefer not to advertise that fact to their friends or family members. Unless someone you know has had a successful short-sale experience with an agent, it may be difficult to get a referral to a short-sale agent from a friend without explaining why.

Ask for a Referral

However, a friend can refer you to an experienced real estate agent. You do not need to tell your friend that you ultimately plan to do a short sale. Just ask for a referral to a competent and experienced real estate agent. If that agent does not handle a lot of short sales, he or she undoubtedly will know who does and can refer you to an appropriate agent. Many agents do not like to do short sales. They believe it is too much work, not enough money (after the lender squeezes the commission), and since there is no guarantee the transaction will close, it could be a lot of work for no money at all.

Agents who like to do short sales are typically quite successful in this venue. They tend to get a lot of short sales accepted. Many agents will also pay the referring agent a referral fee, so it may be any agent's best interest to refer you to an expert short-sale agent.

Find an Agent Online

Because first impressions can be misleading and because so many real estate agents promote their Web sites unrealistically, it is a definite challenge to find a good short-sale agent by looking online. Some agents will fill their Web site with articles about short sales, but they have never completed a short sale. They may call themselves specialists when the truth is they just passed the real estate exam. I hate to say that they lie to you—because they do not see it as lying; they view it as proactive marketing—but the truth is they lie.

You do not need a lying real estate agent. You need an experienced short-sale specialist. Most agents who post blogs and articles online know that many people use a search engine to find certain terms. They will intentionally insert the words that you will search for into their articles, which will push up the ranking in Google but have nothing whatsoever to do with their competency. Their goal is to make you call them and hope that you will not ask too many pointed questions.

With a little investigative work, you can find out who the short-sale agents are in any community. One Web site I frequent is ActiveRain.com. More than 100,000 real estate professionals maintain profiles and blogs on ActiveRain. Use the search function. Enter the words "short sale" and "name of your city/neighborhood." You will find a ton of blogs written by agents in your area about short sale. Click through the blogs to find agents who talk about *negotiating* and *closing* a short sale. You want to meet those agents—the ones who are actively involved in short sales and not just yakking in general about short sales.

Attend Open Houses

Go to open houses, and talk to the agents on duty. Ask the agents who handle a lot of short sale listings. Ask if there are any short sales in your neighborhood, and go visit those homes. Write down the listing agent's name, and look up that agent online.

Look on MLS

If you have a friend in the real estate business, ask this person to pull up all the short-sale listings in a given area. Many MLS provide a search function for short sales, if they do not already require a category status for short sales. For example, in the Metrolist MLS, which serves Sacramento among other cities, an "active short sale" is a category. This helps agents immediately identify a short sale among the sea of other listings.

Sort through the short sale listings by ZIP code to determine which listing agent's name is attached to the bulk of those listings. Then, look at that agent's Web site to determine how many short sales that agent lists. An agent with a huge volume of short-sale listings might not be the best agent for you. What? You might say. Don't you want to hire the agent with the most short sale listings? Maybe not. That agent might be too busy to give you personal attention.

Now that I have addressed finding short-sale buyer's agents, let's look at how a seller can choose a short-sale listing agent.

Choosing a Short-Sale Listing Agent

First, find out how long these agents have been in the business. With a sale as complicated as a short sale, you want to work with an experienced real estate agent. An easy way to get this information is to go to Arello.com, which is a Web site operated by the Association of Real Estate Law Officials. Enter the agent's name and state and click on the R (for REALTOR) button. That should give you the agent's license number. This site does not maintain accurate information for license inception date. You must check the license number against the state records.

To do this, go to your favorite search engine (I use Google.com) and enter the name of your state, followed by "real estate license." Generally, the first site to come up will be the state regulatory division or commission. Go to that site, look for "license verification" or "look up license," enter the agent's license number, and you will find a ton of information about that real estate agent.

A large percentage of real estate agents never make it past their first license renewal. They drop out of the business before then. The reason you want to find an agent who has been in the business for a while is because agents who renew their license time and time again are often those who are making money. Those who are making money are doing more than a handful of transactions per year. With every transaction, an agent picks up invaluable knowledge based on what happens in that transaction. No two transactions are ever alike. You want an agent who can predict a problem and prevent it from happening and an agent who has dealt with problems in the past. Experienced agents will offer you that knowledge and expertise.

When you have narrowed your list to the top three short-sale listing agents, make an appointment with each of them to view your home and discuss his/her marketing plan with you. Use this opportunity to interview the agent as well. Here are some sample questions to ask:

How do you market your short-sale listings?

The agent should do more than put the listing into MLS. You want an agent who will expose your home to the largest pool of buyers as possible, and today that pool of buyers is online.

What percentage of your short sales do not close?

An agent with a high percentage of closed short sales is successful, versus an order taker who cannot negotiate nor actively market their listings. Ask the agent to describe for you his or her worst short-sale experience. Everybody has horror stories.

How workable is my lender?

Some lenders have a bad reputation and, frankly, they deserve it. However, what a bank agreed to do last year and what a bank may do this year could be two entirely different things. The point is you want to determine if your agent has worked with your lender's loss mitigation department in the past. If the agent has experience with your bank, that is a plus, but I would not refuse to hire an agent because she or he has not had dealings with your bank before.

What makes you different from other real estate agents?

Sharp agents know the qualities and characteristics that separate them, set them apart from the competition, and can immediately tell you what makes them different. They should be ready to explain what their strengths are and how they capitalize on those strengths.

Why would a bank accept a buyer's offer for a short sale on my home?

Listen carefully to the answer. The correct answer is because the list price the agent suggests is what your home is worth in today's market. There are other reasons but none as strong as listing it at or below the comparable sales and expecting it to sell at that price.

This is not the time to hire the cheapest real estate agent you can find. All real estate commissions are negotiable, and agents can charge whatever the market will bear. For a short sale, you want full service and a full-service real estate agent. Because the bank is paying the commission, whatever amount is agreed to in the listing agreement will most likely be renegotiated with the bank. So, do not spend a lot of time hassling over the agent's commission, and whatever you do, do not hire a discount real estate broker who will offer limited services or expect you to perform part of the agent's job.

This is also not the time to insist on a higher sales price.

If your home is listed over market value, over the comparable sales, it is highly unlikely that you will receive any offer at all, much less any showings. You want to sell your home as quickly as possible, not *test the market.* The longer your home sits on the market, the less desirable it becomes. Buyers might believe there is something wrong with your home if it is on the market too long.

On top of that, if your price is not attractive enough, buyers will not insist on seeing the home. You will already be at a disadvantage if your MLS designates your home a short sale. That is because many buyer's agents do not send short-sale listings to their buyers, and they try to discourage buyers from pursuing short sales. You might ask, "Why would an agent not want to show a short-sale listing?"

Reasons Some Buyer's Agents Do not Like Short Sales

Short sales take too long to close.

Personally, I have never closed a short sale in thirty days. It is virtually impossible to do. I do not foresee any way that banks will streamline the process in the near future, either. Some short sales can close within six weeks, but some can also take six months or a year. The average length of time for a short sale is about two to three months.

Agents do not get paid until the home closes. If they have a choice between pursuing properties that can close in a normal thirty-day window, many agents will push their buyers to write offers on homes that do not involve a short sale. It is not ethical, and it is not fair, but many agents are eager to get that paycheck, especially, if they sell very few homes and their paychecks are few and far between.

There is no guarantee the transaction will close.

Unless the listing agent has confirmed with the bank that a short sale is possible, you will not know if the bank will consider a short sale until you submit an offer. Agents typically do not contact the bank at inception because the bank will most likely not tell them how much it will take. It is a little bit like asking a regular seller, "Hey, will you take $10,000 less?" A seller will say, "Put it in writing, and bring me an offer." Until the written offer is on the table, there is no offer and there is nothing about which to talk. Banks are not any different.

A buyer's agent can spend two months working on a short-sale transaction before he or she may discover the bank will not accept the short sale. That is two months of negotiations, time, and effort expended for nothing in return. When a buyer submits an offer directly to a seller who is not involved in a short sale, the turnaround time for an offer acceptance (or rejection) is generally twenty-four hours to a week, not sixty days.

The commission might be reduced.

Agents are not supposed to be motivated by money, but let's face it—money is what makes the world go around. I have heard of a few unethical agents who sort the properties they are planning to show buyers by the amount of commission that is offered to them. All broker co-op commissions vary from each other. The listings that pay a higher commission or bonus to buyer's agents often sell very quickly, so you have got to ask yourself, *why is that?*

Of course, many agents never even glance at the commission and, on a whim, could not tell you which of their transactions pay less. There are a lot of honest and ethical agents in the business, and a few rotten apples can give everybody a bad name. However, be aware that it might be difficult for buyers to know which agents put their income second and a buyer's interests first.

Some banks will pay a traditional commission to the listing and buyer's agent. As of this writing, however, most do not. Because all commissions are negotiable and because the bank, not the seller, is negotiating the commission, the amount of the commission in the listing agreement may be reduced. As a regular business practice, my office, for example, splits the commissions with the agents who represent short-sale buyers. However, some real estate offices do not. In fact, some offer a lower percentage split to the buyer's agents.

Therefore, not only will the total commission most likely be reduced, but also the listing broker might refuse to split the commission with the buyer's agent and offer instead maybe 30% or 40% of the commission. Now, the buyer's agent is really taking a hit financially, and some will not do it. For example, say the hypothetical listing commission on a $100,000 home is 7% between the seller and listing broker, and the broker offers 50% of that commission to the buyer's broker. The listing broker would earn $3,500, and the selling broker would earn $3,500.

If the bank renegotiates that commission to, say, 5%, and the listing broker offers the co-op at 40%, now the selling broker would receive $2,000. That is a significant difference from $3,500.

As a short-sale seller, you have the right to insist that your agent split the commission with the buyer's agent or (perhaps pay the buyer's agent more than the listing agent) to entice more agents to show your home. A listing agent probably will not point it out to you, but the verbiage concerning co-op splits is in your listing agreement. As a seller, *you* decide how the commission is to be divided between brokerages. However, alas, many sellers do not read what they sign.

13

Pricing the Short Sale

When you have selected an agent with whom you feel comfortable—an agent with short-sale experience whom you can trust—it is time to pick your sales price. Take off your seller's hat, and put on your banker's hat. Obtain a list of the comparable sales in the neighborhood from your agent, and sort by grouping the sold REOs (bank-owned homes) and short-sale homes into one list and the regular seller-to-buyer sales in another.

Compare the average sales prices and median sales price of the distressed sales to the regular sales. You will most likely find that the sale prices of the distressed homes are lower. The average sales prices are obtained by adding up all the sales prices in a given category and dividing by the number of homes sold. The median sales price is the halfway point where half the homes cost more and half cost less.

If you have very few sold sales, the median sales price will carry less weight. For example, if there are three comps, the middle price will always be the median.

Look at the days on market for each listing. The homes that sold the fastest were the best priced. This is the price point where you want your home to be listed. Ideally, you also want to list your home close to the bottom. However, if fifteen homes sold, and fourteen of those homes sold within one price range, those are the fourteen home prices to use, not the home that was lowest priced. That is because the bank will throw out the odd comparable sale from the group and discard it as an unusual sale.

Next, find the history of each comparable sale—when it last sold and for how much. Soon, you will probably find a pattern. You may see that twelve of the homes sold, say, in 2005 at a median price of $500,000, and that same group sold in January of 2009 at a median price of $250,000. Figure out the percentage of original sales price to distressed sales price on each property. You may discover that 90% of those homes recently sold between 45% and 50% of original sales price in 2005.

If you bought your home in 2005, consider how much you paid for it, and take that number times the average percentage rate. You can use this strategy when you present an offer to the bank to substantiate why your home is now worth 50% of your original sales price.

Next, ask your agent to call the listing agents of the homes that are pending or are active sale contingent. These homes most likely will be sold comps when your offer is received. Pending sales show which way the market is moving. Are prices going up or down? Ordinarily, listings do not reflect the actual sold price until they close, and the accepted sales price may be above or below the listed price. Some agents are not authorized to disclose the final price, and some have no restrictions and will do so willingly. Some agents do not know what they are doing and will spill the beans without knowing whether they are authorized to disclose the sale price. It is worth it to call them and ask.

Finally, pull the numbers for the active listings on the market. Your potential buyers will view these listings when they are also looking at your home. How do you stack up against these homes? Again, look harder at the *active short sale* listings because these are the listings that more closely mirror your actual situation, and you want to align your listing with similarly priced homes. Ask your agent to take you out to tour these homes. Take photographs of them, which you can later use to substantiate your pricing strategy.

When the bank argues with you or your agent about the offer you receive, saying the home down the street was in worse condition or needed repairs, you will have photographs to submit that show the interior of those homes. Banks are not privy to this information, and condition of the home makes a huge difference in the final sales price. You want to give the bank every reason to say "yes" to your short-sale offer and make it easy for the bank to issue acceptance.

When you examine the sold comparables, try to find the original sales price and determine how long it was on the market before the seller lowered the price. How many of those listings had a price reduction and how many price reductions? It is common to find that every listing has had a price reduction. Do not put yourself in that category. You want to list your home at a price that will sell, not at a price that will require an adjustment. When buyers see a price reduction, they assume the seller was greedy and now desperate or something is wrong with the home.

If most homes have a price reduction after thirty days, then examine how long it took after the price reduction to sell. If the period was, say, fifteen days, then price your home a few thousand below the average comparable short-sale price. Do not assume that a buyer will pay your suggested sales price, however. Most buyers want to negotiate.

For some reason and maybe it is the selling agent's fault, buyers rarely look at comparable sales when they make an offer. They look at only those homes that are presently offered for sale. They will say, "Oh, but the home down the street is listed at X amount, and this is so much less! It's a steal." Then, they conveniently forget their gushiness and will discount that price even further, reasoning that you are desperate and do not understand how the market truly works. You have no control over what a buyer may offer. However, you do have control over making your sales price reasonable and attractive to a buyer.

Therein lies the danger of pricing your home too low. In strong seller markets, there is no such thing as pricing a home too low. That is because a low price will bring multiple offers. Multiple offers often drive up the price to ridiculous levels, and it is a small part of the reason we have so many foreclosures today. It feeds on the nature of people to bid beyond what a home is worth because everybody wants it, which means the winning offer often is astronomical and out of the ballpark.

However, if the bank sees your price is too low for the market, the bank may decide that you did not try hard enough to sell at market value and instead opted to give away the house at the bank's expense. This will annoy the bank. When banks are annoyed, they will not approve your offer or consider anything else you have to present. Under these circumstances, you will lose credibility, especially, if buyers submit lowball offers based on your asking price. This strategy can backfire.

Underpricing works well only in highly desirable areas. A home in the Sacramento neighborhood of Land Park was listed in the summer of 2008 around $350,000. It had originally sold at $750,000. The strategy worked because buyers and their agents knew the actual value of this home. It attracted multiple offers, and many were above the list price. Bear in mind the list price was fabricated. It was not real. The winning offer was around $550,000—still, a great bargain.

Marketing Your Short Sale Home to Buyers

Status: Do You Disclose It Is a Short Sale?

Some Multiple Listing Services require that agents enter the status of the listing into MLS, and they will have established a category for Active Short Sale. A status tells other agents whether the home is for sale, off the market, withdrawn or canceled, expired, in contract, in contract but back-ups accepted, back on the market, among other categories. You care about the status because many agents select "status" as a qualifier when they send listings as an automatic e-mail to their buyers.

Some agents will uncheck the "Active Short Sale" box when they set up automatic searches for buyers, which means some buyers will not receive your listing if it is entered into MLS as a short sale. This does not mean the buyer might not find your listing online at another Web site, though. For example, even though the Metrolist MLS that serves Sacramento qualifies short-sale listings, that qualifier does not transfer to every Web site. Trulia.com, for example, does not differentiate short sales, unless the agent puts comments in the remarks section to that effect.

A sample comment that would tell a buyer the home is a short sale is "subject to third party approval." Of course, not all buyers know what that means. Moreover, Realtor.com buries the status under property features, which means buyers might gloss over it. Zillow.com listings do not provide a status for short sales. Zillow status choices are "for sale," "pending," "sold" and "no longer for sale." Again, unless the agent specifically states the home is a short sale in the marketing comment section, buyers will not be notified.

Many short-sale listing agents do not want to disclose to online buyers that the listing is a short sale, unless they are specifically required to provide the status. They would prefer to pique the buyer's interest and entice the buyer to call them. When buyers spot a cute house and a low price, they often will call the listing agent directly. Of course, before the buyer writes an offer, the listing agent will be required to tell the buyer the home is offered at a short sale, but by that time, the buyer will be in love with the home. Once that emotional attachment is made to the home, most buyers will not refuse to write a short-sale offer.

If the buyer is already working with an agent, the buyer might instead call that agent and ask to see the home. The agent will pull up the listing in MLS and, if the short sale status is noted, will inform the buyer of that fact. The agent might try to dissuade the buyer from looking at the home, but if the buyer insists on seeing it, the agent will be required to comply with the buyer's wishes or turn the buyer over to somebody else.

If the listing is not noted as a short sale, savvy buyer's agents will check the property profile or tax rolls to find the original loan amounts secured to the home, and that will tell them it is a short sale. However, many agents do not bother with pertinent details until the buyer wants to write an offer.

What all of this means to a short-sale seller is your listing agent must target both the buyer's agent and the buyer. The agent can target the buyer directly online. However, the buyer's agent is another hurdle to jump. The best way to target a buyer's agent is to include comments in the confidential agent section of MLS that will encourage the buyer's agent to show the home.

First, it helps to let the buyer's agent know whether the listing agent has short-sale experience. A buyer's agent cannot talk to the banks. The listing agent contacts the bank and negotiates the short sale. The buyer's agent needs to feel confident that the listing agent is capable of actually closing the transaction. The listing agent could say, "Don't be afraid of a short sale. I do all the work and close 100% of my short-sale listings."

If the short-sale listing agent has gathered all your documentation, the listing agent might also note in the agent comments, "Short sale package complete and ready for submission." Sometimes buyers submit offers, and by the time the bank approves them, the buyer has moved on to buy a different home. If that happens to you, your agent could then note, "Short sale approved by bank." Banks generally do not see these comments in MLS. Only agents have access to these confidential remarks. However, agents should never write anything in the public marketing comments that would cause the bank to reject a short sale.

Photographs

Buyers love to look at photographs. If there is no photograph, most buyers will pass on that listing and gravitate instead toward listings with photos. It is a crime not to put a photograph into MLS or online, and guilty agents should be handcuffed and forced to watch reruns of *The Gong Show*. Agents who do not publish a photograph are doing a grave disservice to their clients. You have most likely heard that a picture tells a thousand words, and it is true. No picture also tells a thousand words, too, and every one of those one thousand words is bad.

Crisp, sharp, attractive photos are a necessity. If a photo shows an unfavorable feature such as telephone lines overhead, dying vegetation, a home three feet away, ask your agent to crop it. Do not ask to airbrush or to alter a photograph because that would be false advertising, but ask your agent to keep unwelcome elements out of the photos.

Good photographers do not shoot into the sun and shoot with the sun behind them. Your agent might experiment with different angles and various heights. A photo shot from the ground looking up at the home from the corner might give it an entirely new dimension and perspective. Have you ever seen a photo of a home where it is nothing but grass and driveway upfront and way far off in the distance is the little dot that looks like a house? Many monitors are 15 inches or so, and that type of photo might as well be painted black for all the detail it provides. The pros shoot tight pictures.

Here are photography tips for you and your agent:

Walk through your home with your agent and point out interesting elements. For example, wood floors with inlays, fireplace mantles, leaded-glass windows, light fixtures, high-end appliances, custom cabinet hardware—all the million little features that you appreciate and value—show them off, and ask your agent to take photos of them.

Always include several photographs of the kitchen. Buyers place a great deal of importance on the kitchen, and if a listing is missing photos of the kitchen, buyers subconsciously wonder what is wrong. Do not make buyers feel uneasy by omitting photos they expect to see. Clean everything off the kitchen counters, put away the sponges, and polish the appliances.

Arrange flowers and plants in pleasing locations. Try your hand at staging by propping up a gourmet picture cookbook open to a colorfully illustrated recipe. For example, try grouping together a few brightly colored vegetables such as red peppers, yellow squash, and purple eggplant assembled in front of a bottle of olive oil. Keep it simple and classic.

Take photos with the lights on and the lights off. Shoot with the flash on and off. Choose the best ones. Sometimes a camera flash will brighten an area by wiping out detail. Experiment by climbing up a ladder and taking pictures from the top looking down.

Do not miss a single room in your home. In living rooms and bedrooms, open the blinds. If your home sits too close to another home, shoot away from the window. In bathrooms, always close the toilet seat, for crying out loud. Do not stand in front of a mirror, and whatever you do, do not let your photographer include any of your pets in the photos. Some buyers will not consider a home where pets live, and there is no reason to advertise that fact in advance. Let buyers find out you have pets *after* the buyers have fallen in love with your home.

Go out in the backyard, and take photographs at different times of the day. Morning light is very different from sunsets, and you want to avoid casting shadows in your yard. It is understood that you will have put away the garden hose, mowed the lawn, and removed every scrap of personal belongings. You want to highlight your beautiful yard and landscaping, not draw attention to your lawnmower or kid's bike.

Then, ask your agent to drive around the neighborhood and take photographs of the parks, lakes, interesting or well known buildings, nearby schools, libraries, restaurants, bike trails, fountains—aspects of your neighborhood that you want to show to potential buyers. You know your community better than anybody does—show it off. You have no idea whether buyers who are unfamiliar with your neighborhood will be looking online at your home. Paint a clear picture for them through photography, and let them see it through your eyes.

Virtual Tours

It is inexpensive to produce a virtual tour, but the listings that buyers linger on all have them. You will increase the odds that a buyer will want to see your home in person if your agent provides a virtual tour, because buyers do not trust photographs alone, especially, those shot with a wide-angled lens that make rooms appear bigger than they are.

An agent who has never ordered a virtual tour should Google "virtual tours" to find a bazillion companies that offer them. Ask other real estate agents for recommendations. Then, choose the type of virtual tour that you feel will show that home the best, as there are various types available.

Some homes display best by an actual video. Videos generally cost a little more, and they typically include a narrative description of each room. In Sacramento, I like to use a company owned by a famous News 10 reporter. He has that deep voice, and his writing is magical, weaving emotional allure into each paragraph that instantly transports buyers to another place and time. I have no affiliation with his company, but it is called Sunday Open House. He charges around $300 for a video, complete with script and sound. If you and your agent choose video, make sure a professional produces your video. This is not a do-it-yourself job.

Other types of virtual tours include those where a viewer can control the screen by mousing. Simply by clicking on various parts of the room, the virtual tour will move from the ceiling, to the floor, to the walls. Another type of virtual tour uses still photographs and incorporates a feature that zooms in on each room, making the photos appear to move (but do not), then the photo fades into the next photograph.

Probably the most widely used virtual tours are 360-degree tours. To create this type of tour, the photographer secures a camera to a tripod in the middle of the room and then slightly rotates the camera to shoot a series of photos in a circle. Then, the photos are strung together to create a 360-degree effect, which will span the room all the way around. One can also add music and/or narration to a 360-degree virtual tour. Tours can include two spins, four spins, six spins, or more, depending on how many areas of the home are suitable to produce on film.

Signage

Of course, all sellers want a huge honkin' sign in the yard. Whether the agent attaches a sign rider that reads "pre-foreclosure" is a personal preference. Some sellers do not want the neighbors to know that their homes are going into foreclosure, and others do not care. For the sellers who do not care, advertising the home as a pre-foreclosure is a big plus. It makes buyers think they will get a great deal and, who knows, maybe they will. REO agents use this type of advertising for their listings, except their sign rider says "bank-owned." It generates sign calls and activity.

Make sure the sign in your yard contains not only the agent's office number but also the agent's cell phone number. Too many times, buyers call the office number only to find the office is closed. Without a cell phone number, some buyers give up too easily.

If your home has a feature that sets it apart from other homes on the street, ask about hanging another sign rider. Popular sign riders are "Four Bedrooms," "Pool," or "Remodeled."

Make sure the sign is not obscured. Even professional sign companies can mess up on sign placement. Often, I have had to call the sign company that installs my company's signs and ask for sign reinstallation. The sign might be hidden by a tree, blocked by a telephone pole, or placed in a spot where cars typically block the view from the street. If it is a corner property, put a sign on each street. Unfortunately, if you live in a complex governed by homeowner association rules, you might not be allowed to put a sign on the property and instead will need to rely on inside window placement.

If you live on a street that receives little traffic, consider asking a neighbor whose home is located in a prominent spot if you can put a signpost on the neighbor's property with an arrow pointing toward your street. If the neighbor refuses, you might ask about renting the space for your agent's sign.

When I had to sell a condo a client inherited from his mother, I discovered that the HOA prohibited signs on the association grounds. I left a note for the owner of a single-family home down at the corner of a busy intersection, explaining that the seller's mother had died, how he was in mourning, and needed to sell quickly. The neighbor wholeheartedly obliged and let me install a gigantic For Sale sign with a huge arrow directing traffic to the condo development. When I took another listing in that complex, I just left the sign up until the second condo sold. My bad.

Open House

Unless your street gets no traffic, try to have your home held open at least once to see how it goes. Oh, you will hear agents bellyache about holding open houses, and many say they do it simply to appease the seller, claiming homes never sell at an open house. It must be a regional thing, though, because I have sold many homes from open houses.

For example, I once owned a home on Nokomis Avenue in Minneapolis in the early 1990s. I had been thinking about selling it for a long time and was nearly finished getting the home ready for market. Then, one Sunday, a neighbor across the street had an open house. I watched his agent put the open house sign in his yard and noticed that many cars were pulling up and stopping. That is because agents put open house signs with directional arrows on them all around the neighborhood, particularly on busy streets to divert that traffic to the home.

I thought to myself, "Holy Toledo, free traffic!" So, I dusted off an Open House sign in my garage and stuck it in my yard. This led to an avalanche of buyers, and one of those buyers stayed behind after the others left to say he wanted to write an offer. We signed a purchase offer at my dining room table and closed about four weeks later.

Depending on the year, anywhere from 20% to 30% of my listings sell at an open house in California. In part, California buyers consider real estate almost a religion. Many feel that going to an open house on a Sunday afternoon is a regular activity such as going to church or having a Sunday brunch. Moreover, some decide to buy on the spot, even if they were not thinking about buying a home. They might be driving by and see the open house sign. "Oh, Jerry," his wife might say, "I've always wondered what that home looks like inside. Let's stop." And the next thing you know, they are signing a purchase offer.

It helps to *work* your open house. Your agent does not want to make visitors feel overwhelmed by following them around or make them uncomfortable by directly trying to sell them the home. When I greet visitors, I shake hands, announce my name, hand them a flyer, and then give them a brief overview of the home. It might go like this, "Hi, welcome to the open house. My name is Elizabeth Weintraub." This is the point at which they will tell me their names. If they do not, I will say, "And you are?"

"It's a pleasure to meet you. Here is a flyer." I generally hand the flyer to the wife, or I might wave it front of a couple to see which one grabs it. The person who snatches the flyer from me is the person on whom I concentrate. Then, I highlight some of the home's features. I might say, "This is a four-bedroom Tudor. What kind of home are you looking for?" I try to engage the visitors in a conversation. Whatever they tell me, I use in my brief presentation, and I highlight the features of the home that match their desired search. Then, I let them go through the home and leave them alone.

When they come back into the living room, I ask them, "So, what do you think?" (I do not ask yes or no questions.) If they say they love it, I ask them if they could see themselves living in the home and probe for urgency and commitment. If they respond that the home does not quite suit their needs, I will ask them why. For example, they might say they wanted a separate dining room and not a dining area off the family room. Then I will show them how another room in the home could be turned into a dining room. If they do not bite on that, when the next couple comes through, I will bring up the fact they could use an adjoining room as a formal dining room if they so desired.

Your agent should thank them for coming and remind them that if they have any questions, to call. If your agent is courteous and polite, they will remember your home when a coworker, neighbor, or friend mentions they are looking for a home. Real estate agents do not discount neighbors who come by because they, too, might know somebody who would be a perfect fit for your home.

I happen to like holding open houses on Sunday afternoons from 2:00 PM to 4:00 PM, but twilight opens on a Thursday evening draw well, too. If you hold an open house and nobody shows up, then your home is probably not a successful candidate for an open house. However, if you get a lot of traffic, ask your agent to hold it open the next weekend, too, if it has not already sold.

Marketing Your Short-Sale Home on the Internet

You will note that I have not mentioned advertising your home in the newspaper. That is because many major daily newspapers are moving away from classified advertising in print. If your paper contains very few homes for sale, it means real estate companies and sellers believe their advertising dollars do not return enough buyer calls to make spending the money worthwhile. However, almost every newspaper will sell advertising online. Check with your local newspaper to determine its online rates and submission deadlines. Generally, your real estate agent will pay for online advertising for you.

Agents are known for writing an eye-catching headline. Think about the features of your home that make it unique, and ask your agent to play up those features. Stunning Spanish Beauty will attract more buyer calls than, say, 3-bedroom in Sacramento. You know your home better than your real estate agent does. If you can put together a list of every amenity and feature, the results of that effort will help your agent to create fabulous marketing copy.

It is time consuming to upload photographs to many Web sites, but it is important for your agent to submit as many photos as the site will allow. Realtor.com "showcase" listings, for example, allow twenty-five photos, which bumps up the ranking. More photos equal higher placement.

Agents can add a banner and scrolling text, too, so the listings will practically pop out on the monitor. I like to add photos with the most pizzazz first and upload photos of the surrounding neighborhood toward the end, finishing with a photo that will leave a lasting impression. Each of my photographs contains a caption, even if it is something simple such as "dining room," because I do not like to leave buyers wondering, "Just what IS that room?"

There are a bazillion Web sites online where agents and/or sellers can post listings. By the time you read this, there could be a gazillion. Some of the more popular Web sites are as follows:

- Realtor.com
- Trulia.com
- Zillow.com
- eBay.com
- Craigslist.org
- Yahoo.com
- Frontdoor.com
- Googlebase.com
- Vast.com
- Hotpads.com
- Oodle.com

Moreover, do not discount your agent's company Web site or the agent's personal Web site. You might want to consider buying a domain name for your home address and making that a Web site where buyers can view the listing. You can go to godaddy.com and buy a domain name for less than $10. The Godaddy Web site will also provide hosting services if you or your agent is not working with a company that hosts.

Choose an easy-to-remember domain name. If your home is located at 1400 Main Street, I would suggest buying "1400Main." That is because you can advertise the Internet site on a sign rider and on flyers or direct mail, places where buyers may not remember the entire name. They will not recall if it is a street, avenue, or way, but they will remember the URL, if it is simple.

It is easy to overlook details in a listing. Sometimes, we agents fill out so many forms and create so many flyers that a simple detail can be missed. Insist that your agent supply you with the Web site addresses where your home is advertised so you can double-check the content. For example, most listings will contain the following information:

- Property address (the days of expecting buyers to call to get the address are long gone)
- Sales price (you will be astonished at how often the price is missing; it is the driving factor)
- Configuration (number of bedrooms, baths, and types of other rooms)
- Square footage (this is typically listed as per assessor or an approximate size because there have been too many lawsuits filed over square footage)
- Age of the home (if it is an unattractive age, also add its remodeling date)
- Location (near a lake, on a greenbelt, next to a forest)
- Size of lot (can you fit a pool in the backyard, or is it postage-stamp size?)
- Number of stories or levels (include whether it has a basement)
- Amenities, upgrades, features, parking, etc. (promote the best features that make your home sound better than others do)
- Contact information (whom to call for more information or an appointment)

There is no acceptable place to list the fact that the home is a short sale. Buyers purchase based on needs and emotion when they search online. Now, granted, some will be searching for short sales, but as of this writing, they are rare. Most buyers know that REOs can close a lot faster than a short sale. My advice is if you do not have to advertise the home as a short sale, do not.

14

Submitting Short Sale Offers

Last year, an agent on the East Coast posted in his blog a classified ad from an FSBO (for sale by owner) who was trying to sell on a short sale. The ad read in part, *"Buy this short sale so cheaply that you can brag to all your friends about stealing this home. No Realtor commissions."* It made me wonder if the seller had any idea what he was doing. Apart from forking over the bucks to advertise his home, which an agent would have paid for, perhaps this was the reason the seller was in foreclosure. He may not know how to handle his money nor his real estate.

Since the bank, not the seller, pays the real estate commission, about what else might this seller be in the dark? Do you think he knows how to submit an offer to the bank? Would you trust him to submit an offer and negotiate for you? Probably not.

An experienced short-sale agent knows what the lender wants in the short-sale package because the agent has handled many of these transactions in the past. Moreover, agents always call the bank before submitting an offer to find out exactly what the bank wants. Some banks have different demands, but you cannot go wrong assembling all the paperwork that you know in advance the bank is likely to request and then adding the additional documents requested.

Writing a Short-Sale Offer

The listing agent will typically guide the buyer's agent to write the offer correctly. Some buyer's agents do not close more than four real estate transactions a year and might not be familiar with all the little nuances that can go into a short-sale offer.

While purchase offers can be written on the back of a cocktail napkin and be a legal and binding agreement, most states utilize a standard and commonly accepted purchase agreement. Some are issued by the state's association of realtors. An attorney can draw the purchase agreement, too. In California, for example, the standard form is the C.A.R. California Residential Purchase Agreement and Joint Escrow Instructions, commonly referred to as the RPA. Our agreements consist of eight pages and a two-page Buyer's Inspection Advisory.

Here are the elements of California's purchase agreement. Your state contracts might vary.

The date the purchase agreement is signed is generally the same date as it was prepared, but the dates do not need to match. However, the date the agreement is signed should be after the date it was prepared and not before that date. It states a few specifics such as the city in which the offer was signed, and it identifies the property address, its assessor's parcel number, and the county.

The most important element, of course, is the purchase price offered by the buyer, followed by the financing terms. It lays out the earnest money deposit, to whom it is payable, the form in which it is payable (cashier's check, personal check, cash), whether it is to be held uncashed, and where it will be deposited upon offer acceptance (into escrow or the broker's trust account).

The bigger the earnest money deposit, the stronger a buyer's offer will appear to the bank. It makes the buyer seem serious and committed. Your state purchase agreement will clarify in the body of the agreement whether the earnest money deposit is refundable and the terms under which it may be returned to the buyer.

Next is the financing. Banks will want to know the amount of the loan, which will reflect the loan-to-value ratio, and the type of loan, whether it is conventional, FHA, VA, etc. To figure the loan-to-value ratio, take the loan amount and divide it by the sales price. For example, a $240,000 loan divided by a sales price of $300,000 results in a ratio of 80%. That means the buyer is putting down 20% and obtaining an 80% loan, which equals 100% of the sales price.

Regardless of whether the buyer is putting down 5% or 20%, it is still all cash in the end to the bank, yet banks (and sellers) believe the buyer with the bigger down payment is a more qualified buyer. It is generally easier for a buyer with 20% down to qualify for a loan than it is for a buyer, say, with 5% down. That is because the banks maintain tighter guidelines for buyers who are putting down 5% because that type of loan is considered riskier for the bank.

The exact date of closing, or number of days to closing after the offer is accepted, is important to the bank. If an offer specifies sixty days or longer, the bank might not be as receptive to the offer as it will to an offer that promises to close within thirty to forty-five days. Possession—the date and time the buyer may occupy the property—is negotiable. Sometimes buyers will give the sellers a few days to move after closing, and sometimes they demand possession immediately upon closing. In California, the closing (not possession) is determined by the time and date the deed is recorded in the public records. In other states, closing takes place when the money changes hands, and it could take weeks for the documents to record.

The area where some buyer's agents get into trouble when writing an offer is when specifying the fees and expenses the bank will agree to pay. In special situations, the bank might agree to pick up certain seller fees, but generally, the bank will pay for very little.

Typically, banks will not pay for a pest report. If the buyer asks for a pest report and agrees to pay for the pest report, it is highly likely that the buyer's lender will ask that the buyer pay for all the recommended work and will demand a pest completion certificate. If the buyer does not want to be obligated to pay for a pest completion, the buyer might want to consider leaving the pest report out of the purchase agreement. This is a topic to discuss with the buyer's real estate agent, mortgage lender, and real estate lawyer.

Some banks will refuse to pay for a natural hazard disclosure (NHD), yet California state law says the buyer is entitled to an NHD. In that event, the real estate agents often will pick up the cost of that report to make sure the buyer receives it.

The entity that pays for title insurance and/or escrow is the entity that chooses the service. In Sacramento County, it is customary for the seller to pay for title insurance and escrow. However, in Placer County, right next door, it is customary for the buyer to pay for the owner's title insurance policy. Sometimes the escrow fee is split between the seller and buyer. The short-sale banks I have worked with on Sacramento real estate, however, do pay 100% of the title insurance and escrow fee.

Other costs such as transfer taxes and HOA document preparation fees are negotiable. The buyer's agent should ask about all the fees in the contract before writing the purchase offer to try to keep the offer as clean as possible. That is not to say you cannot negotiate, but the answer is likely to be no, and the bank will probably refuse to pay for a home protection plan as well. Somebody has to pay the fees that the bank refuses to pay, and all eyes will be looking at the buyer.

If a buyer asks for personal property such as the refrigerator, washer and dryer, or furniture, the buyer's lender will want an addendum clarifying that the personal property is not part of the purchase contract. That is because banks do not want to finance a dining room table. When including personal property in a purchase offer, it is considered wise to specify that the personal property conveyed be without warranty and without consideration. In other words, the seller is giving those items to the buyer without any guarantees and for free.

California purchase contracts, like many contracts in other states, specify that the buyer is purchasing the property in *as is* condition. However, many banks are unaware of this clause, so it might be a good idea to draw it to the bank's attention by stating it on a separate line in the contract. After all, the seller cannot pay for anything to be repaired, and the bank is unlikely to pay for repairs as well, so just spell it out to ease the bank's anxiety. You are not giving up anything that is not already in the C.A.R. purchase agreement.

About now, you might be asking about the home inspection. Is the buyer entitled to conduct a home inspection? I chortle a little because it is a bit like asking, is the Pope Catholic? Not only are buyers entitled to a home inspection, they are told fifty ways from Sunday to get a home inspection. Do all buyers pay for a home inspection? These days, most of them do. The ones who do not are the buyers who are crying after the escrow closed that defects were not disclosed.

Although sellers are required to disclose material facts in California, they are not required to do so in all fifty states. Proving that a seller intentionally withheld information from a buyer is tenuous at best. A buyer's best protection is to obtain a home inspection from an individual qualified to perform such an inspection. Contracts are generally contingent upon certain inspections, and a home inspection is one of them.

However, a home inspection is only as good as the inspector hired. As with most services a person pays for, one can hire a good home inspector or a bad home inspector. In some states such as California, home inspectors are not licensed. This means anybody with a tool belt can print business cards proclaiming to be a home inspector. I suggest buyers hire a home inspector with experience, training, and membership in a home inspector's association, the latter of which at least guarantees the inspector is exposed to new regulations.

Should a buyer hire the home inspector recommended by a real estate agent? See, I knew you were thinking about this question, so I asked it for you. The answer is, "it depends." I will not deny that some agents use inspectors who will not blow the deal for them. It happens. There are unprofessional agents in the business just as there are unqualified home inspectors.

However, most experienced agents recommend the best home inspectors available. That is because the agent truly wants the buyer to receive disclosure and to make an informed decision about whether to buy a home that has defects. Let me say, though, that all homes have defects, even new homes. If a buyer is concerned about the quality of a home inspector, that buyer should ask to see a sample home inspection report before hiring that inspector. If the report is a few pages, a buyer should cross that name off the list. Reputable home inspection reports are exhaustive and lengthy, comprising thirty pages or more.

My recommendation is to make a short-sale purchase offer contingent on a home inspection. If major defects are found, such as the home is sliding down the hill, the buyer might want to reconsider pursuing the short sale.

Purchase contracts also contain a disclosure and confirmation of agency relationships. If the seller is represented by an agent, it should be noted, just as the buyer's agent is noted. However, if a short-sale buyer has signed an Exclusive Buyer Broker Contract with the buyer's agent, realize that if the buyer's agent works for the same brokerage as the seller's agent, the contract is now subject to dual agency.

C.A.R. contracts give an agent permission to operate as a dual agent as long as the buyer signs. Always read your contract. If you desire legal advice, ask a real estate lawyer to interpret the language for you because real estate agents cannot give legal advice. Real estate agents can say, "I need your initials here and here and here." However, they cannot tell you why. That is because they are not lawyers. Do not sign anything you do not understand without legal counsel.

A purchase contract typically contains contingencies,

items that if not satisfied or fulfilled mean the buyer has the right to cancel the contract. Common contingencies are appraisal, loan, and investigations. Some contracts contain provisions that give buyers more rights, but lenders rarely turn down an offer because they contain contingencies.

Even though a buyer may believe the price of the home is fair, always ask for an appraisal contingency. The lender authorizing the short sale will get its own comparable sales, maybe hire an agent to prepare a BPO (broker price opinion), or run the property through its desktop appraisal software; however, the buyer's lender will require an appraisal. If the property does not appraise at the approved short-sale price, with an appraisal contingency, the buyer has the right to walk away or renegotiate.

A loan contingency gives the buyer the same right to cancel if the loan cannot be obtained. Buyers might be tempted to waive the loan contingency, particularly if the buyer is relatively assured of obtaining the loan; however, the future has this funny little way of being unpredictable. Employers can go bankrupt at the drop of a hat or a buyer could be fired or hit by lightning; you just do not know. Loan contingencies can run with the entire contract to closing, or they might be removed within a certain number of days.

Investigation contingencies let buyers examine the home by hiring professional inspectors: home inspectors, pest inspectors, roof inspectors, sewer inspectors, and so forth. The expense of these inspections is borne by the borrower because the short-sale lender will most likely refuse to pay for them.

Included in the investigation contingencies are reports and disclosures from the seller, preliminary reports or title commitments, and other such matters pertinent to each locale such as natural hazard disclosures, the latter of which are required in some states. If an inspection or report turns up a serious defect, the buyer can ask the short-sale lender to pay for it but realize that if the lender refuses, the only recourse left is to walk away from the sale.

Whether the deposit is returned to the buyer if the buyer walks away depends on the contingency verbiage in the contract. Most contracts allow for the return of the earnest money deposit to the buyer within the contingency period. However, if the buyer cancels the contract after removing all of the contingencies, it is highly likely the buyer could lose the earnest money deposit if the buyer cancels at the last minute.

The liquidated damages clause in a contract generally limits the amount the seller is allowed to retain. C.A.R. contracts limit that sum to the actual amount paid as an earnest money deposit, up to a maximum of 3% of the purchase price. If the contract price for the home was $300,000, for example, and the buyer put down $15,000 as an earnest money deposit, in the event of default, the seller would be required to return $6,000 to the buyer. If the buyer put down $1,000 and defaulted, the seller could claim $1,000. That is why sellers often ask for larger earnest money deposits.

Buyers are not required to sign a liquidated damages clause. It is voluntary. However, California contracts require initials by both the seller and buyer to be enforceable.

Arbitration clauses are also common in contracts. By signing an arbitration clause, both the buyer and seller agree to settle disputes by hiring an arbitrator without taking the matter before a court of law. In C.A.R. contracts, issues such as earnest money deposits that fall within the guidelines of Small Claims Court do not require mediation. Some people like to duke it out in court and will refuse to sign away their rights to a trial by jury or judge. As with the liquidated damages clause, initialing arbitration is voluntary and requires both the buyers' and sellers' initials to be enforceable.

Sometimes, disputes can arise in a contract during the contingency period. A buyer might find fault with the property in some manner and decide to cancel the contract. This is why it is rarely advisable to put down an earnest money deposit in excess of what a buyer can afford to put at risk. Earnest money deposits are not automatically refunded without the signatures and agreement of all parties. Take the case of Susan and David. The seller wanted Susan and David to make an earnest money deposit equal to 3% of the sales price and issued a counter offer demanding an increase from $1,000 to $9,000 on a $300,000 sales price.

Susan and David's real estate agent advised them to increase the earnest money deposit after the contingencies were removed. The seller agreed. However, during the contingency period, Susan and David discovered the home had mold in the basement and decided against asking for remediation of the mold. Instead, they decided to cancel the contract.

The seller disputed this claim and demanded the earnest money deposit. By signing the arbitration clause, the buyers mistakenly thought they had to agree to mediation. However, the disputed sum of $1,000 fell within the scope of Small Claims court. Susan and David filed suit in Small Claims, and the judge returned the deposit to them, plus interest. If they had deposited the full $9,000, that sum would have been outside the jurisdiction of a Small Claims court in California, and all parties would have had to go through arbitration.

Finally, a purchase contract should set a deadline for offer acceptance and specify how the accepted offer will be delivered. C.A.R. contracts, by default, state the contract will be deemed revoked if not signed and delivered to the seller by the third day at 5:00 PM. These contracts also let the maker of the contract specify a different entity for delivery such as the real estate agent. At any point prior to this date and time, the buyer may withdraw the offer.

So, say, buyers Mary and Jeff make an offer to buy a short sale from Linda and John. They state the offer is good until February 4 at 6:00 PM, and receipt by the buyer's agent is deemed delivery. If Linda and John sign the offer on February 4 and deliver it to Mary and Jeff's agent at 5:00 PM, the sellers cannot withdraw the offer at 5:59 PM because it has been delivered and accepted. However, if the offer needed to be delivered to Mary and John in lieu of the agent, Linda and John can cancel at any time prior to actual delivery.

Sometimes, short-sale sellers reconsider, or sometimes, they can receive a higher offer after accepting a lower offer and want to cancel the contract they signed earlier. That is when the designated party for delivery and the time for delivery become important.

C.A.R's Short Sale Addendum spells out exactly how long the buyer will give the short-sale lender to accept the offer. It specifies when the earnest money deposit will be deposited, and at which time the investigation periods and contingencies commence. It is not necessary that a buyer submit the SSA with the offer, but a buyer would be foolish not to. If your agent's realtor association does not have such a form, it would be wise to ask a lawyer to draw one for you or include those provisions in the original purchase contract.

In conclusion, buyers are generally required to initial every page of the purchase contract, including certain clauses such as liquidated damages and/or arbitration, and then sign in full on the last page. The agent representing the buyer signs the contract as well. Often, additional pages will follow, such as a buyer's inspection advisory or supplemental advisories/disclosures.

Make copies of the accepted offer, and keep the originals. Do not let your agent send the original purchase contract and/or addendums to the bank. If the bank insists on original inked signatures, sign two copies, but always keep an original copy for yourself or your agent.

There is a good reason to submit the purchase offer without the seller's signature. I believe it is better to submit a fully executed contract to the bank, but sometimes the listing agent might have already submitted such an offer, and the second offer cannot be fully accepted by the seller due to the previous acceptance. In this situation, just include the purchase offer without the seller's signature, and let the bank choose among the multiple offers.

Buyer Qualifications

The documentation submitted on behalf of the buyer needs to show beyond any doubt that the buyer is qualified to purchase the property. Say the bank has postponed the trustee's sale or halted the foreclosure proceedings while the bank considers the buyer's offer. The bank wants assurance that the buyer is in a position to close the transaction. Sometimes, being in a strong position to close carries more weight than, say, a few thousand dollars difference in price.

Never submit an offer that is subject to obtaining financing without a preapproval letter from the buyer's lender. A preapproval letter says the mortgage broker or lender has reviewed the buyer's credit and verified income and assets. It states that, based on that information, the buyer has been preapproved for the loan.

This is different from a prequalification letter and is stronger than a prequal letter. A prequalification letter says the mortgage broker or lender has taken a loan application and believes the borrower qualifies to buy a home. The mortgage broker or lender has not verified income or scrutinized assets and may not have pulled a credit report. The letter implies that as long as the buyer's loan application checks out and is correct, without any surprises, it is likely that the buyer will be qualified to purchase the property.

Now, given those two choices, which type of letter do you think a short-sale lender will want to receive from the buyer's lender? If you want to present a more powerful preapproval letter, obtain such a letter from a representative of the short-sale bank, and submit both preapproval letters. A buyer is free to choose the lender, regardless of which lender issues a preapproval letter. By submitting both letters, a buyer is saying, "See, even your bank has approved me; I am getting the loan from my own lender, which has also approved me. I am fully qualified."

Not all mortgage brokers follow the same procedures for preapproval. That is why a preapproval letter from the short-sale lender's representative is important—because the short-sale lender knows how the preapproval was obtained and trusts its direct lending representative to provide a truthful and accurate picture of the buyer's finances. In addition, if the short-sale lender wants more information about the buyer, it is all there in the file of its own representative.

The preapproval letter should state the amount of loan for which the buyer is preapproved. There is no reason to submit a letter reflecting an amount higher than the offer price. If the bank believes a buyer is qualified to pay more, the bank might ask for a higher sales price. Of course, if the buyer was preapproved through the bank's employees, the bank has access to the buyer's application and can determine the top dollar the buyer can afford to pay, but few go to that trouble. There is simply no sense in telling the bank that a buyer could easily pay up to $400,000 when the buyer is offering $300,000.

Submit a copy of the earnest money deposit check to the bank. The check can be payable to the real estate company, a lawyer handling the transaction, a title company, closing company, or escrow company. Typically, it is not cashed until the bank accepts the offer. The higher the earnest money check, the beefier the offer appears. The mere fact the earnest money deposit is mentioned in the offer is not sufficient. The bank will want to see a copy of the check.

In some situations, a buyer letter is warranted. This letter should explain in factual terms why the buyer should purchase the property. There is no emotion in this letter, unlike the appeals buyers might make to a regular seller with a heart. The bank and its investors have no heart. They care solely about their bottom line and reducing the impact on that bottom line.

Do not disclose anything that is unnecessary or does not build a solid case for offer acceptance. Stick to the facts. For instance, here are some facts the bank would like to hear:

1. The buyer has the available cash for a down payment and does not need to sell another home to purchase this home.
2. The buyer can quickly close, say, within twenty-one to thirty days.
3. Disclose the buyer's mid FICO score to the bank, but only if it is above 720.
4. Upon acceptance, the buyer will shorten the investigation/inspection contingencies.
5. The buyer will pay some of the seller's fees and accept the property in *as is* condition.

Property Condition Letter

Note to Real Estate Agents Concerning an Agent's Visual Inspection

It is becoming increasingly popular for listing and selling agents to prepare a visual inspection document and obtain the sellers' and buyers' signatures on this document. Some agents mistakenly believe the California AVID (Agent's Visual Inspection Disclosure) is an inspection that is supposed to disclose defects, similar to the agent's contribution to the TDS (transfer disclosure statement); however, that is not the purpose of an AVID.

The AVID is a visual inspection of each room and the exterior of the home. For example, an inspection of a bedroom would state the type of floor covering, whether the room has baseboards and/or molding, the type of light fixtures, number and placement of receptacles, size of closet, whether the door latches when closed, door hardware, types of window coverings and number of windows. It is a complete picture of the room without the photograph.

If the home has defects, these can be listed on a separate sheet and attached to the AVID. Be specific and detailed. If the carpet is worn and has stains, note that and provide an estimate (from a reliable source) to replace the carpet. If the kitchen is missing an appliance or windows are broken, list those, too. Add up all the repairs that detract from value, and provide a fix-up cost to repair or replace those items. That value can be deducted from a comparable sale value and be used to justify the short-sale offering price.

Photographs will build a case as well. The lenders are not inside the home to look at its condition, and a BPO will not clarify the condition either if the agent has not been inside. Many times, agents drive by a home and judge it by its exterior, which could be very misleading. If you decide to include photographs, do not print out digital photos. Put the digital photos on a CD, get them professionally developed, and label each of them with the property address, loan number, seller's name, and room description. Get double prints, just in case the bank loses the photos.

The greater number of defects that are identified and documented, the better the chances at getting the short-sale offer accepted. Banks are aware that if the home goes through foreclosure proceedings, the condition of the home could change. Sometimes, sellers will rip out the kitchen cabinets, sell the appliances, and destroy the property before moving out.

Preparing an Estimated Closing Statement

Sellers and their agents can prepare an estimated closing statement themselves, but it is far more practical to ask an escrow officer, closing officer, or real estate lawyer to prepare it instead. The preferred document is called a HUD-1, which is a standard settlement statement established by the Real Estate Settlement and Procedures Act (RESPA) for closings involving federal mortgage loans. HUD stands for U. S. Department of Housing and Urban Development.

It is similar to preparing a tax return because preparing a HUD-1 settlement statement can make you want to tear out your hair and sob. It lists all the charges and credits, the money coming into closing and the money going out, and provides a final net figure for each of the parties. In the case of a short sale, the last line on the seller's side on page 1 will be a minus number.

The bank will be more concerned with the fees charged to the seller than those charged to the buyer. The buyer can pay anything a buyer wants, including interest-rate buy-downs on the new mortgage and even a home protection plan, but the seller cannot contribute to those fees.

Line 401 is the contract sales price. This is the amount the buyer hopes the bank will accept and the amount the buyer is proposing to pay for the home.

The rest of the 400 numbers apply to fees the seller/bank has paid in advance or will pay in advance and may contain a prorated number for property taxes on Line 407. The bank will pay typically very few fees in advance, outside of property taxes. The prorated portion is the amount the bank will be credited for time the seller will not own the property. For example, first-half taxes in California cover the period from January 1 to June 30. A transaction that closes on March 30 would involve a credit to the bank/seller for taxes paid from March 30 to June 30. Adding up the 400 number credits will equal a gross amount due to the seller/bank that will most likely exceed the offered sales price.

Line 502 involves reductions in the amount the seller will receive, which is derived by adding the amount of settlement charges on the second page of the HUD-1. These fees generally include Line 703, which is the total amount of the commission paid to the listing and selling brokers.

Line 1100 fees are related to title charges. Line 1101 is the closing or settlement fee paid to the closing company. There may be other title search fees found on Lines 1102 to 1104, a doc prep fee on Line 1105, notary fee on Line 1106, and an owner's title policy fee on Line 1110. Whether the bank will pay for an owner's title insurance policy depends on local custom.

Line 1200 fees are government recording and transfer fees. City transfer tax and county transfer tax can amount to a big chunk of change. In California, county transfer tax is computed on 55 cents per $500 of sales price.

The 1300 line fees are additional settlement charges. Line 1303 is for payment of county taxes. If, say, a California transaction closes on March 30, escrow may collect the full six months of taxes due from January 1 to June 30 from the bank. That is why there may be a credit given for the unused portion on line 407. Typically, banks will refuse to pay for any items charged on any line item 1300 fee except for property taxes. The total amount of settlement charges from line 1400 is then entered on Line 502 as settlement charges to the seller/bank.

Of course, the biggie in all these fees is the payoff to the bank. Until the bank issues a short-sale demand letter, that amount is unknown, unless the bank has verbally dispatched a number. The number that is entered on line 504 is the payoff amount of the first mortgage. Likewise, if there is a second mortgage, that payoff amount is entered on line 505. Line 520 is the total amount of all the line 500 charges.

The gross amount due the seller/bank from line 420 in entered on line 601. The gross amount of reductions from line 520 goes on line 602. Subtract line 602 from line 601, and that number will be the negative figure, a minus number, that you hope the bank will accept to accommodate the short sale.

Whew! I hope you can see why preparing a HUD-1 might be a task better left to the professionals to do for you. However, by understanding what the fees are and how they are calculated, all parties should scrutinize the HUD-1 before submitting that document in the short-sale package. That is because closers can make mistakes. When overworked, it is easy to transpose a number or mix up a credit with a debit. Nobody has ever worried about the time spent to go over each number on the settlement statement and confirm the accuracy, but many have been sorry they neglected to do so.

After completing the HUD-1, all the documents should be ready for submission to the bank. Here is an overview of the documentation:

1. Authorization letter. This letter can also authorize the buyer's agent to talk to the lender.
2. Hardship letter from the sellers.
3. Comparable sales.
4. Property condition letter.
5. Preliminary title report/commitment.
6. Purchase offer and addendums.
7. Tax returns, W-2s, payroll stubs.

8. Preapproval letter from buyer's lender.
9. Copy of earnest money deposit.
10. Copies of seller's bank statements.
11. Copies of seller's assets and liabilities.
12. Copy of the executed listing agreement.
13. HUD-1 settlement statement.

To download free samples of the above documents, go to TheShortSaleSavior.com and sign up for the free Short Sale Savior report. You will receive a link to your free documentation kit that includes sample letters.

Make a copy of the entire file before submitting it.

Call the bank's loss mitigation department, and try to get the name of a person to whom you will send the file. Often the loss mitigation department will not assign the file to a negotiator until a person or the department reviews the file. Banks are reluctant to give out the name of an individual, and instead, they will say, "Just send it to loss mitigation." Agents should ask, "To whom am I speaking, please?" Then, address the package to that person.

The answer may be "No, we all work together," but send it to that person anyway, along with a sub-address of "loss mitigation." In addition, agents should get the direct phone number or that person's extension number. Do not ask if you may have it because that requires a yes or no answer, and the answer might be no. Say, "Oh, and I need your direct phone number." Follow it up with, "And what is your FAX number?"

Fax the complete package to the bank to the attention of that person in loss mitigation as well as sending the package via overnight delivery. The following day, your agent will call and ask if your fax has been received, perhaps ask if the overnight delivery has been received. The next day, the agent will call to see if the package has been reviewed. It will not have been, but agents should call anyway. Then ask how many files that individual is handling and be understanding, empathetic.

If an agent is lucky enough to talk with a person who seems friendly, say you understand what a heavy workload and stress under which they must be. If the bank's loss mitigation employee will engage in a conversation, he or she might remember your agent the next time he or she calls.

Once the file has been reviewed, it will be sent to a negotiator. Your agent will spend most of the time trying to reach this person for the next month or so. Negotiators are swamped. I do not know of a single negotiator with time on his or her hands. Many try to process five hundred files or more per month, and it is almost humanly impossible to do so. Your agent should get the direct phone number of the negotiator as well as the toll-free number.

Then, try to get a timeline for the file. Some negotiators will come right out and say that it will not be reviewed for a certain period. If your agent is told to wait two weeks, then your agent should mark his or her calendar and start calling that 14th day, very early in the morning, right when the bank opens. When the agent receives voice mail, and you know your agent probably will, your agent should leave a cheery, happy, and brief message. Call back just before lunch. Leave another pleasant message. Call again before everybody goes home.

If your agent is on the West Coast, for example, and the bank is in New York, your agent may need to call the bank at 4:59 AM PST, again at 8:59 AM, and again at 1:29 PM or 1:59 PM, depending on when employees leave for the day. One can find out their hours by asking loss mitigation when they work.

Sometimes, negotiators will let their voice mails fill up with messages, meaning no more messages can be left until they clear out their voice mailbox. Do not think they do not do this on purpose. If nobody can get through to leave a message for them, they do not have to worry about calling anybody back, you know. Pretty sneaky, huh?

I have had that happen on more than one occasion, so it is not a fluke. It is a practice. Smart agents do not hang up when they hear the voice mailbox is full. Instead, they stay on the line to see if there is an alternate number given on the recording. If not, they press zero. Zero will often take a caller to an operator. If there is a number or extension, ask your agent to call it. Then, ask if the negotiator is working or is on vacation.

When I called a negotiator who had pulled the full voice-mailbox trick on me, I dialed the extension. I called that extension so many times that I often would get a person I had spoken to before. That is because I keep a transaction log. I make a note of the day and time I called, the person's name I spoke to, and the number I called, plus a brief recap of the conversation.

Rebecca, let's call her, answered the extension. She recognized my voice and asked how I was doing. I asked her how she was doing, working in a department where callers yelled at her all day long. Then I explained my problem—how I could not get through to the negotiator and the close of escrow was but days away. If we did not close, the buyer would walk away. Rebecca was sympathetic. "What do you want me to do?" she asked.

"I want you to get up out of your chair and walk down the hall to see if (let's call him Dan) is in his office. I will hold the phone and wait for you." I was astonished, but she did as I asked. Yup, Dan was in his office. I asked her to tell him she was going to transfer the call to him and to plead with him to pick up his phone. Fortunately, Dan took my call, and within a few minutes, he approved the short sale.

If I had not pushed, that file would still be sitting in limbo, and the buyer would have grandchildren by now. Sometimes, all it takes is that one extra little effort to get the file approved. Agents should not take no for an answer, but do not be sarcastic, threatening, or nasty to anybody at the bank. Your agent will get much further with honey than vinegar. Well, I did mention that I write for About.com, which is owned by The New York Times, and would be doing a story on my short-sale experiences. However, I did not say it in a mean way. Then, just for good measure, I added, "I'm sorry, what was your name again? How do you spell it?" Being a journalist carries weight in some circles, and so does blogging. Blogs reach a national audience.

Agents should be creative. Be positive. They should never allow anger or frustration to consume them because it will not serve the purpose. The goal is to get through to the decision maker, to find out what additional information is required and when a response can be expected. Squeaky wheel gets the grease is one of my favorite mottos. I continue to call until I am connected to an individual responsible for approving the short sale.

In all fairness, it is often not one person who will approve the short sale, though. Sometimes it goes to a committee. Personally, I think committees are the worst because everything takes longer when a meeting is scheduled and a consensus must be met. Each individual has his or her own agenda. There are personality clashes among ego trippers, brownnosers, and worse, all coming together at one table. Trying to satisfy everybody is impossible, which is why most decisions made in committees suck, but I digress.

Files can also require submission to the bank's investors. Depending on the day and time, you might get an opposite response than you would have received a day earlier. If investors are making money, they are happy. When they are losing money, they are unhappy. Some days are better than others are. For many in the banking business, it is a matter of survival and cutting losses before it is too late—and for some, it was too late last year.

The Long Wait for Short-Sale Approval

Felisha and Steven, not their real names, called me late one evening about a short sale. Her sister, Maria, referred Felisha to me. I had helped Maria and her husband buy a home in the same vicinity where Felisha and Steven wanted to move. This home had been on the market for several months as a short sale, and I could easily see why. It was the highest priced home in that neighborhood.

Felisha knew the home because her sister was a close friend of the sellers. When her sister told her she might be able to buy the home for hundreds of thousands less than the mortgage, Felisha's eyes lit up. This was her dream home, and she insisted on buying it. The decision was partly impulsive and partly a smart financial move. Felisha and Steven lived across the river in West Sacramento, and their smaller two-bedroom home was paid for—they owned it free and clear. They wanted to pursue the listing because this was a remodeled home of almost 3,000 square feet in a nicer neighborhood, and it would put them closer to the family.

The sellers of the home were in the midst of a not-so-friendly divorce. To add to the drama, the listing agent and Mrs. Seller were not on the best of terms. Mrs. Seller was in the middle of trying to fire her listing agent when I showed up at the home with Felisha and Steven. The listing agent, we will call her Edith, refused to cancel the listing because she had already submitted two short-sale offers to the bank.

Fortunately, Mrs. Seller favored selling the home to Felisha and Steven, since Felisha's sister was one of Mrs. Seller's best friends. The problem was winning over the listing agent. From the listing agent's point of view, the less time she spent talking to Mrs. Seller, the better. In addition, the listing agent had two offers in the works and did not really want to submit another offer, especially, from an agent she did not know.

I spent almost an hour on the phone talking to Edith and listening to her rant and rave about Mrs. Seller and agreeing with her—not that I had any reason to believe any of the accusations but because I wanted Edith to cooperate and submit an offer from Felisha and Steven. I did not care if the accusations were true or fabricated. It was not my job to take sides in this battle. It was my job to help my buyers purchase this home.

During the course of my hour-long chat with Edith, I found out how much the other two buyers offered, which was tremendously useful information for Felisha and Steven. Multiple offers are always a tough battle, but it requires even more finesse when it is a short sale because most buyers do not want to overpay for the home. Most buyers hope to purchase a home for far less on a short sale. It rather makes up for the hassle they have to go through to get the home.

To say this home had been extensively remodeled would be like saying ice cream is cold. It does not quite describe it. Mrs. Seller designed the kitchen and family room by copying it verbatim from a movie. Did you ever see the 2003 film, *Something's Gotta Give*, with Jack Nicholson and Diane Keaton? Mrs. Seller fell in love with the kitchen in that movie and decided that kitchen belonged in her home. She duplicated the flooring, the white cottage cabinets, the granite counters, and the hanging light pendants, including buying an exact replica of the sink, faucet, and all the appliances. It was eerie, and it cost her plenty.

She did not stop there, either. She added a second floor to this older ranch home. For the master bath, she turned to a Restoration Hardware catalog and copied an advertisement. This massive room was painted a trendy grayish-green. It had marble floors, a walk-in shower, separate clawfoot tub, recessed lighting, and the vanity, which featured marble counters and double sinks with brushed-nickel faucets, ran from wall-to-wall. The master suite walk-in closet was large enough to be used as an extra bedroom.

Mrs. Seller poured, at best guess, more than $200,000 into the home, which she secured by taking out a second mortgage. The home towered over everything else around it. It was a white elephant. "If you buy this home," I warned the buyers, "You can never move again. It will never go up in value like the other homes around it."

We wrote the offer for a little under $500,000, and Edith submitted it to the bank on Valentine's Day. Almost three months went by. I called Edith at least once every couple of weeks to see how things were progressing. The notice of default was filed in February, so we had time to wait. In California, foreclosures take roughly 3 ½ months.

As we were nearing the wire for the trustee's sale, Edith called. It turned out that both of the other buyers who had submitted offers had decided to increase their offers. Edith suggested a price increase. I should add here that Edith had no authority to disclose the prices of the other offers to anybody, but that did not stop me from asking. In addition, Edith did not know that Felisha's sister was also talking to Mrs. Seller about the offers. I told you there was drama.

By the end of the third month, Felisha and Steven had increased their offer to $518,000. This meant the second lien holder would still take a bath. The first mortgage lender, however, decided to give a little something to the second lender. We sweetened the deal by telling the bank we would close within twenty-one days without any contingencies. Within a week, Felisha and Steven were approved for the short sale, and they won the home. When a short sale happens, it happens fast.

Mrs. Seller, on the other hand, was not ready to move out. She asked to rent back for several months. Felisha and Steven, because they were grateful, were considering letting her stay. "Think about it," I cautioned. "If Mrs. Seller can't make her mortgage payment, what makes you believe she's a viable candidate for a tenant—do you want to be a landlord or a homeowner?" In the end, we closed on a Friday, and Mrs. Seller agreed to give the buyers her brand new front-loading Neptune washer and dryer if she could stay through Sunday.

Felisha and Steven moved into that $750,000 home and

received almost a $250,000 discount, including a new washer and dryer. They had waited four months for the short-sale approval and successfully won the battle of multiple offers. They were emotionally exhausted. I never asked if they ever rented the DVD of *Something's Gotta Give* and paused the film to examine the kitchen, but I imagine they did. I would be tempted, wouldn't you?

Not All Buyers Are Willing to Wait for a Short Sale

Charlie and Renee (not their real names) are a good example of a patient couple that tried to wait. They have long-range plans to raise a large family and wanted to buy a big house in Natomas, a Sacramento, CA, suburban community of homes built in the early 2000s to the present. They hired an inexperienced agent to help them find a four- to five-bedroom home.

At the time, the neighborhood values had fallen about 50% due to the housing slump and influx of foreclosures. Many buyers who purchased homes in Natomas had utilized 100% financing. When home values fell—coupled with fixed-rate mortgages turning into adjustable-rate mortgages at that time—many homeowners bailed and stopped making their mortgage payments.

The agent Charlie and Renee had hired did not have short-sale experience. She found them a home that required a double escrow and submitted an offer for them. A double-escrow home is a situation where the listing agent has entered into a contract with the seller at a much lower price. Then, the listing agent offers to sell the home, closing simultaneously, at a higher sales price to a buyer. The listing agent wants to make a profit beyond the commission and likely figures one can jack up the price to cash in on a buyer's ignorance.

How they get this past the short-sale lender is beyond me, because I cannot imagine a lender being willing to eat in the shorts (hence the name short sale) and let the listing agent walk away with a huge profit. To make such a transaction work, the short-sale lender most likely would not know that home was being flipped with a concurrent closing. However, some unscrupulous companies specialize in flipping short-sale homes. To make sure buyers are not caught in this trap, buyers should think twice about buying a short-sale flipper.

Charlie and Renee had waited almost two months for a response to their offer. It was not really the home they wanted, but it was a good price. Not to mention, Charlie and Renee had saved up almost $60,000 in cash and waited two years to for the market to drop. Now that prices had fallen, they saw this as an excellent opportunity to purchase their dream home finally.

Feeling impatient, Charlie and Renee called me. I suggested they let the short-sale offer lie low and look at a few other opportunities. They had not signed an exclusive buyer's broker agreement with their present agent, but I insisted they tell her they were changing agents while still agreeing to let her represent them if her short-sale transaction ever materialized.

I showed these delightful buyers a series of homes over a period of several days. Some were short sales, and others were bank-owned properties, REOs. We narrowed the selection to two homes. One was another short sale and the other an REO. The homes were very similar to each other, about 2,200 square feet with four-plus bedrooms. We wrote two offers on each of them and submitted two separate earnest money deposits.

After ten days or so, we heard back on the REO home. This home was originally listed at $285,000. Charlie and Renee had offered $265,000. The listing agent was unresponsive. We submitted the offer on a Monday morning, and I did what I always do, which was call the listing agent to say I had e-mailed, and FAXed, an offer. By Monday evening, he had not called me, so I sent him an e-mail and left him another voice mail. On Tuesday and Wednesday, I sent two more e-mails and left two more voice mails. Still no response. By Wednesday afternoon, I called his office and asked if the agent was in town. Yup, he was not on vacation.

Thursday morning, I called and left a voice mail for the agent's managing broker. In the most polite tone and cheery manner that I could muster, I explained that I did not want to get the agent into trouble. In fact, I did not need to have a conversation with the agent, and I was not going to ask him how much the bank would take nor inquire about how many offers he had received. The only thing I wanted to know was *did the agent receive the offer from my buyers?*

I hate to say this, but this type of behavior from REO agents is very common. I do not know why banks hire these agents. On this particular transaction, the listing agent was paying a referral fee of 30% to Asset Link for the lead, but that is a more or less standard fee. Therefore, the agent was making a good commission. Why don't they earn it? Because banks either do not care or never hear about this type of behavior, I suspect.

Many REO agents refuse to return phone calls all together. They record a message on their voice mail that essentially says, "Don't call me, ever. I will call you if I feel like it." When they receive offers from buyer's agents, they hand over the paperwork to an underling for submission to the bank. If the bank accepts another offer, the listing agent typically does not bother to call any of the other agents for days, sometimes weeks. The service is unprofessional and unethical.

If any bank wants to know how hard its appointed listing agent is working, the bank should ask a buyer's agent to call and document the response to determine how quickly the listing agent responds or whether the listing agent responds at all. After a few phone calls, I am fully confident that the bank would fire those agents in a heartbeat. It is bad enough the bank has excess inventory it needs to dump, but giving one agent fifty listings to sell is not saving the bank one dime—and it's hurting the industry.

By Friday morning, the home on which the buyers made an offer showed up in the Multiple Listing Service with a price reduction. It had dropped in price from $285,000 to $265,000, which was the exact price my buyers had offered. Why? It made no sense. I could think of two reasons why the bank might have done this. First, it may have wanted to encourage multiple offers in hopes that other buyers would offer more than $265,000. Second, the right hand at the bank might not have known what the left hand was doing. This happens more than you would imagine. Departments do not communicate with each other.

Five days later, on a Tuesday, the listing agent's managing broker returned my phone call. He apologized for the listing agent's failure to contact me but offered no reason as to why it took *him* five days to call me back. I let that small annoyance slide. I was simply glad to be talking to a person at the brokerage who might be able to tell me if the buyers' offer was received eleven days ago.

While I had the broker on the line, I made a suggestion. Some listing brokers will send a FAX when an offer has been received to let the buyer's agent know it has been submitted to the bank. It is a form fax with a place for the property address, the date the offer arrived, and the date it was sent to the bank. The fax also explained how the process would go, which was again, "Don't call us, we'll call you when we feel like it." In any case, it takes all of two seconds to fill out and slap on a FAX. It is so simple; the listing agent's underling could do it. The broker appeared receptive to that idea.

The managing broker then promised me that the listing agent would call me within the hour. Fifteen minutes later, the listing agent was on the phone. Yes, he had received my offer. Well, thank goodness for small miracles. Then he told me the strangest story.

The bank had received many offers. One of the offers was all cash and for more than list price. The all-cash buyers had offered $290,000 on this $285,000 listing. My heart sank. My buyers had offered only $265,000 with 20% down to a conventional loan. I envisioned their offer going bye-bye into the circular recycling bin.

But wait. Do you remember that price reduction to $265,000? Apparently, when the all-cash buyers saw that price drop online, they freaked out. They figured something was seriously wrong with the property. You know what they did? They withdrew their offer! My heartbeat increased.

When the bank agreed to accept the all-cash offer of $290,000, the other buyers had slinked away. Now, there were no offers on the table except the offer from my buyers. Talk about timing!

However, the agent explained, the bank did not want to look at any offer that did not include a preapproval letter from its approved lender, and that letter must include the mid-level FICO scores. The listing contained a provision telling buyer's agents to call a certain loan rep for preapproval. We had tried calling that loan broker when we first submitted the offer. The buyer called him five times on that Monday, but the person never called him back.

Therefore, my resourceful buyers located another loan rep who worked for the same bank at a different branch, and we received a preapproval letter from her. She was slow as molasses, and although she claimed several times to have e-mailed the preapproval, I had not received it nor had the buyers. I immediately called the loan rep and asked her to verify with the buyers that it was all right to release their mid-FICO scores and then send me the scores contained in a new preapproval letter.

"I can't do that," she replied. "Not without verifying with the listing agent that this information is required." Sigh. She did not work for the listing agent. Buyers have a right to request the release of any information they authorize. Besides, what guarantee was there, given my experience with the listing agent, that she would ever reach him? After much bickering, she finally FAXed over the preapproval letter with the mid-FICO scores.

I then resubmitted the offer to the listing agent. Much to my surprise, what did I receive back, but a FAX telling me the offer had been received. Holy Toledo, we can make a difference in this industry. Then, the listing agent called me to say he had received a couple more offers.

I have been in the business long enough to know that sometimes buyer's agents write offers on REO listings, and they never call the listing agent at all. They just figure they can lowball the bank and get it accepted. It was likely those other offers were either all cash and for less than list price, or they came in at one to two thousand over list price with financing. I suggested the buyers submit an addendum increasing the price by $5,000 to $270,000, which they did.

Three days later, the bank accepted their offer. However, it was with the provision that they make their deposit either non-refundable, or they remove all their contingencies. This meant removing the right to inspect the home and waiving the appraisal and loan contingency. If, say, Charlie lost his job the day before closing, he and Renee would be out of luck and forfeit their deposit, which was substantial. Charlie and Renee were OK with those conditions; however, at the very least, I insisted, they should get the home professionally inspected that afternoon.

We called my two top home inspectors, and they were both busy. I then called the third inspector. Although his day was booked solid, he had time in the early evening to conduct a thorough inspection. We set the appointment.

Home inspections are extremely important, whether or not the sale is *as is*. Buyers have a right to be informed and to know if there are significant defects or major repairs required. The home inspector spent three hours combing the property, inspecting the major systems and components, checking every electrical receptacle, turning on the appliances, crawling into the attic, and looking for signs of trouble. He found nothing significant—a few cracked tiles on the roof and an interior door that did not latch properly. The home was clean as a whistle. Whew!

The offer Charlie and Renee had submitted on the short-sale flipper was now still on the short-sale lender's desk. That home was smaller, in a less desirable neighborhood, and they still had not heard back from their previous agent. The REO home had larger square footage; it had five bedrooms instead of three, perfect for their future large family. It was time to cancel that short-sale offer and move forward with the home they truly wanted.

Charlie and Renee closed escrow on the REO home three weeks later. They had waited two years to buy a home. They had waited three months for a response on the short-sale offer. The REO, despite its initial problems, had come together in less than two weeks.

Some Short Sales Close Faster than Others

Pacita Dimicali, an agent with Gallagher and Lindsey Realtors, Alameda, CA, sold one of her short listings *twice* before the deal stuck. Her sellers had originally paid $575,000 for their Spanish bungalow on Roberts Avenue in Oakland, located a couple blocks from Mills College, which they bought directly from the previous owner. This was a pretty, white stucco bungalow with a tile roof and a manicured lawn in an excellent neighborhood.

After two years, the sellers' financial situation changed, and they decided to sell. Based on the comparable sales, however, their property was worth $399,000. Pacita listed the home and finally received an offer of $365,000 on a short sale. She and the sellers waited the usual forty-five days—plus days for a negotiator to respond. The short-sale offer was accepted, and the buyers' inspection period began.

The buyers spent more than $1,000 on various home inspections and found a number of defects. The repair estimates totaled more than $80,000. Because the sellers had originally purchased this home directly from the previous sellers, they did not know they were supposed to get the home inspected at that time and waived the right to an inspection. The sellers were shocked at the amount of repairs the home needed. Sadly, instead of renegotiating, the buyers walked away from the home and canceled the transaction.

Pacita was not about to give up. Armed with the inspections, she asked the negotiator to order a BPO. She handed copies of the home inspections to the BPO agent and requested a price reduction to $310,000. The bank agreed with Pacita's assessment, so she put the property back on market, advertising that the short sale was already approved and available for a fast closing. Pacita immediately received an offer for $299,000 ($100,000 less than her original list price), and the bank accepted the new buyers' offer within twenty-four hours. The short sale home on Roberts Avenue closed three weeks later. Pacita calls this her fastest short sale ever.

As you can see, it can take a long time or a short time for a short sale to be accepted. Pacita had done much of her work in advance, which is why her short sale was approved so quickly. Some buyers such as Charlie and Renee discovered they might be better off pursuing other opportunities while waiting for approval on a short sale. Other buyers such as Felisha and Steven wanted only one house, and if the short sale was not approved, they were not going to pursue another home. For Felisha and Steven, the long wait was worth it. No matter how long the wait, if the short-sale home is your dream home, then you should wait, regardless of how excruciating and frustrating.

15

Bank Negotiations

Before submitting a short sale to the bank, it pays to find out whether the property is in foreclosure. Not every short sale is in foreclosure or needs to be in foreclosure. It is a misconception that homeowners must be in default or behind in their payments before a bank will consider a short sale. In strong real estate markets where prices are rising, typically a homeowner does need to be in default; however, in falling real estate markets, lenders can easily figure out that values have dropped, perhaps placing their security in a precarious position—that is, without equity to support them.

In fact, I closed such a deal in March of 2008. The homeowner had bought a home in the neighborhood of Land Park in Sacramento three years prior when prices were unbelievably high and continued to climb. This seller's problem was he bought a one-bath home. Now, the market was soft. There is not much of a demand for one-bath homes over half a million in Land Park. The seller had drawn up plans to add a second story with a master suite, but that cost would have been out of line for the neighborhood. He would have been better off simply adding a second bath but instead, he remodeled the kitchen.

Do not get me wrong, remodeled kitchens carry extreme value and definitely add to the bottom line in any home remodel. Kitchens are the number one best improvement a homeowner can make. They return the most bang for the buck. However, very few buyers want to spend more than $500,000 for a three-bedroom home with only one bath in a neighborhood where that kind of money will buy them a two-bath home. Not to mention, the seller paid an excessive amount for the home when he bought it. I ran the comparable sales from 2005, and he paid a primo price for that home.

To compound problems, the home had been on the market already for three years, and everybody in the neighborhood knew it. The seller tried to sell it himself for a while, and then he listed with an agent. The price was too high, so it did not sell. After the listing expired, the seller called me.

He gave me thirty days to get that home into escrow. Frankly, the odds were not in my favor, but I decided to try it. The home had plenty of vintage character, but it was empty. Without furniture, the home seemed cold and uninviting. I called Barbara LaSalle, a home stager in Sacramento, and she agreed to stage it at a price below her normal fee. She divided the huge living room into separate spaces, breaking up the oversized room into cozy entertainment areas. Barbara moved a double bed into the master bedroom, making the room appear larger, brought in a dining room table and a kitchen table, and arranged artwork on the walls, which transformed the home from an empty slate into a warm and happy environment.

We set the price about $100,000 less than its last listed price, which brought it more in line with the neighborhood comparable sales. I held several open houses, and the foot traffic was phenomenal. Some buyers came back every weekend to look at the home again. One of them stuck around long enough with his agent that he wrote an offer on day 21.

The offer was very close to list price. The problem was the seller was making payments on two mortgages, both of which totaled more than the sales price. "Don't worry," said the seller. "I have a working relationship with my banker, and we will rewrite the second mortgage into an unsecured promissory note." Bear in mind, the seller was *not* in default. I had my doubts, but the seller was certain he would work out an arrangement with the bank.

We were in escrow for thirty days and nearing the date to close. The seller had not yet reached an agreement with the bank. I could see short sale written all over this transaction, so I asked the seller for an authorization letter to talk with the lender on his behalf. At least the seller had reached the point in negotiations where we had an actual negotiator assigned to the case. Therefore, I had a person I could call—on his direct line. How hard could this be?

Very hard. I had one conversation with the negotiator, and he asked for a HUD-1, which I immediately FAXed to him—and that was the last time we spoke for weeks. During our conversation, the negotiator promised me the file would close within two weeks, that he had every piece of documentation required. I called a few times over the following week and left more voice mail messages. By the second week, the negotiator's voice mailbox was full. It remained full for two more weeks.

Still, I called three times a day—morning, at lunch, and at night. I varied the calling times. I transferred myself to the loss mitigation department after every call and asked for help. After a while, I got to know one of the call center's staffers in loss mitigation.

By day 58 of the escrow, I was becoming desperate because the buyer was threatening to cancel. You see, the buyer did not sign on for a short sale. The buyer thought this was a normal thirty-day escrow, but here it was two months later, and we were still in negotiations with the bank. On top of this, the bank refused to let the seller pay for a few repairs that totaled $2,000. The buyer's agent and I decided to each kick in $1,000 to make the deal work. However, understandably, the buyer was feeling frustrated and antsy about the whole situation.

I put in one more call to the negotiator and transferred to loss mitigation. The woman I had had many conversations with in the past asked how she could help. I explained the entire situation—that the seller wanted to make a deal to payback the shortfall to the bank, this was not an ordinary short sale, and we actually wanted to pay the bank. I guess she felt sorry for me and perhaps tired of my calling so often, so she managed to track down the negotiator and persuade him to turn off letting all calls go to a full mailbox and actually answer my call.

Just like that, without any more delays, the negotiator e-mailed the short-sale demand letter to escrow approving the sale. I looked at a copy of the letter and compared it to the estimated closing statement, and it was $2,000 short. I almost choked. To have come so close to closing, yet be so far away. How could that happen? I knew my chances were very slim of reaching the negotiator again at this point, but I was not the type to give up at the last minute, no matter how dark the skies may appear.

It turned out the negotiator had made a clerical error while preparing the short sale demand. He fixed it, e-mailed the new short-sale demand letter, and we closed the following morning on day 60, the deadline. Wipe the perspiration off my face, why don't you. Since I had picked up the negotiations with the bank on day 30, this was actually a thirty-day short sale, which is incredibly fast. The seller handled the negotiations with the bank after the short sale closed. I knew it was painful for him, so I never asked whether he had promised to pay back the full amount of the shortage, or if he negotiated a lower amount in exchange for saving his credit report, but I would imagine it was the latter.

16

Why Banks Reject Short Sales

You might never know the reason why the bank may reject a short-sale offer because the bank is unlikely to tell you or your agent. I have had bank negotiators slam down the phone on me, offering little more than, *"The answer is no, and don't let the door whomp your butt on the way out."* I take that to mean they did not like the offer. However, the reason for rejection could be any of the following:

Believe Home Will Sell For More as an REO

The biggest reason why a bank would refuse to approve a short sale is price. Bank management, the employees who make the decisions, sit behind closed doors in front of their polished desks, devoid of paperwork, and quickly scan a file, looking for the slightest discrepancy in price. They order desktop appraisals or pay some schmuck a pittance to run a BPO, and from this, they determine value. Occasionally, the bank might pay an appraiser to inspect the property physically, but that is rare.

When I was working on a short sale for a teardown property in Land Park, I met the bank's appraiser at the property. He immediately began talking about how the values for R2 properties were higher in this neighborhood, insinuating that his appraisal would reflect his opinion that it should appraise for more than I had hoped. He had not toured any of the duplexes in the neighborhood. However, he had a list of their sold values, and that was what he intended to use.

I stomped on the floorboards to show they were weak. I pointed out the mold growing along the baseboards in the bathroom. I showed him how the kitchen cabinetry was falling off the walls. He did not care. He was determined to appraise the property for $300,000 when it was not worth a penny over $200,000. I explained that the other duplexes and homes in Land Park did not back up to a gas station, they were not located on a heavily traveled street, and they were not in such disrepair.

The appraiser did not understand the neighborhood and knew it only by reputation. He had no idea how investors would view the property because investors would undoubtedly be the ultimate buyer for such a project. Instead, he appraised it as though it was completely remodeled, and then he deducted his estimate—which was way off—to fix up the place. My gut instincts told me when the appraiser shook my hand goodbye that this deal was not going to fly.

Now, we had been trying to postpone the foreclosure for months. The seller had submitted all the required documentation, escrow had prepared the HUD-1, and we were ready to rock and roll. Every day, I would call the negotiator and ask for the file to be escalated. Every day, the negotiator told me he would check on it.

In the end, the way I found out it had been foreclosed upon was when the new listing agent called me to say he was working with the bank and putting the home on the market as an REO. I called the bank to ask why, and I was told the file was rejected, now shut up, and go away.

That home eventually sold as an REO for $180,000. My seller had an offer at $220,000 that the bank had rejected. I drove by the property after escrow closed. The new buyers had torn it down. They left one wall standing to qualify as a remodel and not new construction.

Missing Paperwork

The next reason a bank rejects a short sale is because the file is incomplete. The agent may have sent all the documentation but not at the same time. You cannot expect bank employees to match up paperwork with each file. Well, you can, but they probably will not do it. If a piece of paper is missing from the file, often the file gets shoved down to the bottom of the pile and forgotten while the bank's employee works on a file with complete paperwork. A complete file has priority.

Your agent might call one day to ask if the paperwork the negotiator requested from you was received, and he is told yes. Then, the next day, the document is not in the file, and nobody knows where it is or if it was received. Therefore, your agent sends it again. If the agent does not call and follow up, you will never know that it was misplaced, even if your agent has received confirmation that it had been received.

On the other hand, a negotiator might say that everything is in the file, take it to a committee meeting, and decide the bank wants another document. That is when your agent will discover yet another unknown requirement had not been fulfilled. It is helpful for your agent to document a transaction log every time he or she talks to the negotiator. The log should note the day and time, to whom your agent spoke, and what was discussed. It might not satisfy the bank because they are unlikely to believe your agent, but at least, it will make both of you feel that neither of you are losing your mind.

When push comes to shove, and it may, your agent should send every document again. Load up the FAX with a cover letter, noting the loan number, and every required document, and push send.

Expect your agent to ask for feedback each time he or she is lucky enough to have a conversation with the negotiator. Your agent should ask the negotiator how the file looks. Is there anything that could strengthen your argument for a short sale? If so, then make sure your agent sends it immediately.

No Short Sales Allowed

A bank might refuse a short sale if it does not intend to allow a short sale in the first place. I am not certain if the bank is being polite, placating the seller and agents, or if it derives some sort of pleasure from inducing hope in sellers and agents only to slam the door in their faces.

Discount Policy

The bank might have a policy of not accepting any offers that are less than 90%, or some other percentage, from comparable sales. Of course, no one at the bank will explain that until your agent has spent countless hours and money putting together short-sale packages and calling repeatedly. It is of no help to learn which banks have this sort of policy because as soon as you find out the bank's policy, it will change.

Sold the Note

As realtor Pacita Dimicali can tell you, sometimes the bank will run you around in circles without disclosing it no longer holds the mortgage. She took a listing from sellers who had originally purchased their home from Pacita's sellers two years ago, but another agent had represented the buyers (who are now the sellers). Instead of calling their agent when it was time to sell, the sellers called Pacita.

Because she did not represent the buyers when they purchased the home, she did not counsel them about their choice of financing. The buyers had qualified for their financing based on *stated income* and 100% financing. Like so many buyers who fell into that trap, they could no longer afford to make the payments because they were not really qualified in the first place to buy the home. Since the market had softened, the sellers now owed more than their home was worth and figured their best chance at getting out from under the mess was to do a short sale.

Pacita immediately obtained all the required paperwork such as the sellers' W-2s, pay stubs, bank statements, financial statements, etc., and asked the sellers to give her a hardship letter and authorization letter for the bank. She sent the paperwork to both the first and second lenders, hoping to begin the short-sale process early.

A month later, both banks called to say that they would look at a package only when the sellers have received an offer. Pacita worked diligently to prepare the home for sale and jumped into action. She persuaded the family of six to vacate the premises, so it would be easy to show and remain in presentable condition. She staged the home, held broker tours and open houses, filmed and posted online a virtual tour, and spent a fortune on advertising.

All that hard work paid off because the sellers immediately received an offer. This time, Pacita made certain every document was in order. She placed each paper into a binder and separated the topics by using colorful tabs, and then overnight expressed two complete packages to both of the banks.

Two weeks later, the first lender called to say it would not approve any short sale because it had sold the mortgage to another bank. At the same time, the second lender called to say it *would* approve the short sale and take 15% of the mortgage to release it; however, it wanted the sellers to sign a promissory note for the 85% difference it was about to release. As Pacita pointed out, if the sellers could afford to pay the shortfall difference, the sellers would not be asking for a short sale.

This meant that even if Pacita was successful at tracking down the new first lender and submitting the short-sale offer to this lender, the second lender was unwilling to cooperate. You might wonder, why didn't the first lender tell the agent or the seller that it no longer held the mortgage for that property in the first place? Your answer would be as good as mine would, I am afraid.

Shareholder's Stock May Decline

While a home is in default, the home remains as security for that mortgage. Not every mortgage that goes into default ends up as a foreclosure. Sellers can reinstate the loan or make up the back payments to stop the foreclosure. However, once a home has been sold on a short sale, the bank takes a stated loss.

If stockholders see too many short sales, they may believe that the bank's assets are not as solid as they may appear. When stockholders lose faith in a bank, they dump their stock. Dumping stock can cause the bank's stock prices to decline.

The Seller Does not Qualify

Banks are not in the charity business. Some banks want the sellers to suffer as much as the bank. If the seller has excellent credit, a strong cash flow, and assets, the bank will want to take all three. Ruining the seller's credit temporarily is not enough blood.

The bank will ask for the hardship letter. If there is no hardship, the bank will most likely expect the seller to make the bank whole, either by paying the difference in cash, selling assets to come up with the shortfall, or agreeing to pay the bank on a promissory note.

For example, say the home will sell for $700,000, but the balance on the first and second mortgages amount to $800,000. Closing costs and commissions could total another $50,000. That brings the total amount to close to $850,000. Now, after subtracting the sales price from the cost to close the transaction, the bank would be upside down. It means the bank would eat $150,000. The bank would look at the seller and say, "Hey, we didn't sign on to underwrite your mistakes. Pay up, or shut up," and the short sale may be declined.

The Buyer Does not Qualify

Buyers who look shaky on paper make banks nervous. If the buyers have no assets, a low credit score, or little cash to use as a down payment, the bank might deny the short sale because it may not believe the buyer will qualify for financing. Even if a buyer submits a prequalification letter with the offer, the seller's lender may not buy it.

Many prequal letters are worth less than the cost of the paper on which they are printed. A prequal letter does not mean the buyer's employment has been verified nor that the buyer's credit necessarily has been scrutinized, let alone been approved by the lender.

In addition, low earnest money deposits can cause a lender to believe the buyer does not have any money. If the bank sees an earnest money deposit of $100 or $500 on, say, a $300,000 offer price, the bank may reject the offer in hopes of later attracting a more qualified buyer. Local custom may dictate how much of an earnest money deposit is acceptable. Where I work, the minimum is $1,000, but the average is closer to 1% of the purchase price for homes above $300,000.

17

Dealing with Two Loans on the Short-Sale Home

The longest short sale I have ever handled took nine months to close. This was the horse property in Rio Linda where the sellers were taken to the cleaners when they bought it, paying close to $700,000 for a home that was to sell close to $400,000 two years later. They used 100% financing to buy it, utilizing the then-popular 80/20 combo loan, which was an 80% first mortgage coupled with a 20% second mortgage.

Fortunately, the buyer was the patient sort and waited while we submitted package after package to the lender. We fought with the second lender tooth and nail to get approval. The lender reluctantly agreed to take $1,000 for its $130,000 mortgage, which the first lender had offered in exchange for a release of the lien.

We sent the estimated HUD-1 statements to both lenders and received them back in record time. Great! We were ready to close escrow. Except, for some reason, the buyer's lender messed up the loan documents, and we had no choice but to send them back to be redrawn. This caused a delay. Because of the delay, the short-sale approval letters expired.

We went back to the drawing board, resubmitted the revised HUD-1 statements, and asked both lenders for updated short-sale letters. The first lender submitted the letter immediately, but the second lender dragged its feet. After repeated phone calls, we were informed that the new short-sale approval letter required approval from the bank's investors. The investors held a meeting and a few weeks later declared that $1,000 was no longer satisfactory, and they wanted more. They wanted $5,000.

At this point, the first lender refused to hand over any more money to the second lender and held its ground—either we figure out some way to satisfy the second lender's demands or the deal could fall apart. Neither of the lenders seemed to care anymore. There was only one way this deal was going to come together and close, and that was if the buyer paid the extra $4,000. I suppose the buyer felt as if she was held hostage and had no choice.

The truth is I do not believe she had any other choice. She had come this far, waiting nine months for the property. You could have a baby in nine months, for crying out loud, and it would be less painful. When the transaction did not close on schedule, we managed to sweet talk the tenant into moving out, and we gave early possession to the buyer, which meant the buyer was already living in the home, along with her horses, and paying rent to the sellers. In the end, the buyer coughed up the additional $4,000, and the transaction closed. But talk about being down to the wire and being beat on the head.

There are several ways to negotiate with the second lender. The obvious, of course, is to point out that if the lender does not cooperate, it will be placed in the position of having to foreclose or otherwise lose its entire investment. Most junior lenders realize that they have no equity, so it does not make sense to bring the payments current on the first and file their own foreclosure because the property will still be upside down if they get title through foreclosure.

In an ideal world, the second would reconvey the mortgage for zero compensation. To gain cooperation, explain how the first mortgage holder is taking a huge loss, and do not be afraid to share with the second lender exactly how much the first lender is losing. Put it in dollar terms, not percentages.

For example, say the first mortgage is $400,000, and the second is $100,000. If the property is now worth $300,000 and closing costs, plus commission, equal $20,000, that leaves $280,000 for the first mortgage holder. The first lender, in this instance, will have lost $120,000. Which sounds like a greater loss—30% of the mortgage or $120,000?

Second, agents need to make it very clear to the second mortgage lender that the seller is not receiving one thin dime out of this sale. Talk about the seller's financial stresses and terrible, horrible events that forced the seller to try to sell as a short sale. Mention the seller's ruined credit report. Paint the worst picture that you can.

You never know, the second might agree to release the loan. However, if those arguments are met with resistance, then your second best option is to ask the first mortgage holder to take a little bit bigger hit and offer the second a small sum to release the loan. Many second mortgage holders would rather take one or two thousand than end up with nothing at all. Most of my short sales are handled in this manner where the first agrees to toss over a thousand or so to the second lender, regardless of the amount of the second.

If none of those arguments works, the last option is to offer the second mortgage holder a promissory note for the balance or a portion of the balance. Bear in mind, the first mortgage holder will need to agree to this. The first mortgage might say, "Whoa, wait a minute, if the second gets a prom note, we want one, too," and that could open another can of worms. Promising to repay the debt in full means it is not really a short sale.

On a sad note, sometimes you cannot do or say anything to persuade a second mortgage holder to release the loan. I am not certain if they want to cut off their nose to spite their face or what the reason is, but some simply will not cooperate. They would rather lose everything than get a little something. It does not make sense, but I suspect you are realizing by now that not all short sales make sense.

It is possible that the second lender may refuse to negotiate and release its loan if the lender is in a position to pursue a deficiency judgment, providing the existing second is a hard-money second and its security for that loan would disappear after a foreclosure. However, it makes little sense to pursue a deficiency judgment if the borrower has no assets. It's a little like trying to squeeze blood out of a beet.

A Nonsensical Short-Sale Tale

Erin Attardi, an executive associate at Lyon's Sierra Oaks office, discovered that not all short sales are awarded to the highest and best offers. Erin has been selling real estate for about two years and received most of her referrals from the Internet. She sold enough her second year to qualify for Master's Club, which is a designation only 6% of the agents achieve. Therefore, when a short-sale listing came along, Erin tackled that job with ferocity because she did not know that real estate was not supposed to be that hard.

She had listed a pre-foreclosure as a short sale in a suburb at $369,000. Within a few weeks, the seller received an offer for $320,000. Erin was giddy because it was her very first short sale. How hard could it be, she thought. She submitted the offer to the bank, along with the requested seller package, and started counting the days.

The buyer was giddy as well because he had just received custody of his daughter, and the school his daughter attended was only a few blocks away from this home. Thanksgiving was just around the corner, and everybody always seems to be in a good mood that time of year. Just as Erin thought she had the deal sealed and ready to go, she received two more offers from other buyers. One offer was at $330,000, and the other was $345,000, both substantially higher than the first buyer's offer.

Real estate agents are required by law to submit all offers, so it is not as if Erin could favor one buyer over another. She did not have the heart to tell the other agent that she had received two higher offers because it would most likely break his buyer's heart to find out that he might not get the house near his daughter's school, but she made the call. Then, she sent both offers to the bank.

By now, it was almost Christmas. The first buyer was understandably anxious. Erin called the bank and braced herself for the bad news. Surely, she imagined, the bank would take the offer for $345,000. However, that did not happen. The bank, in all its infinite wisdom, decided to accept the first offer for $329,000!

You must ask yourself why. I would. All three offers came from well-qualified buyers. The highest offer would have netted the bank an additional $25,000. It does not make sense to accept the lowest offer, does it? The bank said it made sense. The bank reasoned that it had already approved the file from the first buyer. If the bank elected to accept one of the other offers, it would have to start the process all over from square one. Since it was that far along and ready to issue the short-sale approval letter, it decided to let the other two offers fall by the wayside and take the lower offer.

The bank was simply too busy with a backload of other short sales to try to get the highest and best offer for the bank. This transaction closed in early January. Wow! This is fun, thought Erin. This is easy to do. And she could not wait for the next short-sale listing to come along.

By March of 2008, Erin's wishes were granted. She listed a short-sale home in Lawrence Park, a pretty, little neighborhood situated around a park. Almost as soon as the For Sale sign went into the yard, Erin's seller received an offer from a buyer who jumped on it. The buyer wanted this home because it was located directly across the street from her mother.

The first and second loans were held by Countrywide, which had its own unique set of circumstances after merging into Bank of America. During this period, Countrywide was outsourcing its loss mitigation department. Every time Erin called the bank to check on the status, she was directed to a different negotiator. During the first six months, Erin had worked with fourteen negotiators! The excitement and ease of her first short-sale success was beginning to fade.

It seemed to Erin that every phone call resulted in a five-day delay, regardless of what the bank promised her. She never knew from one day to the next whether she would be assigned to a new negotiator or if the negotiator-of-the-day would call her back. Sometime in August, the bank ordered a BPO (broker price opinion), and the file seemed to be back on track. The buyer, on the other hand, had a sixty-day rate lock that was on the verge of expiration.

To speed things along, the buyer made an appointment to sign all the loan documents and deposit funds, which then let escrow send the final HUD-1 to the bank for approval. Four days elapsed. The clock was ticking. However, Countrywide did not sign the HUD-1 nor send it back to escrow. Escrow was threatening to reject the buyer's funding wire, and Erin was ready to tear out her hair.

She called it an Act of God. She called seven to eight times and talked to the short-sale department, the workout department, and the triage department when her call finally landed on the desk of a person who took pity on her. Erin explained the situation, and she was given the supervisor's direct phone number, which she immediately called. She received approval within two minutes.

For a transaction that started in March, this short sale did not close until early December, almost ten months later. But thankfully, it did close. The seller moved to Idaho, and the buyer moved in across the street from her mother, a decision I hope the buyer does not come to regret. Surely, thought Erin, this was the worst transaction ever, but the worst was actually yet to come.

Do you remember when I said that banks do not generally pay for any repairs? That is true. However, every once in a while, a short-sale buyer can get lucky. A beautiful home in the rolling hills of South Land Park was listed as a short sale by the seller's relative. As is typically the case with a part-time agent, the home was overpriced. During the listing, the seller received an offer, but the buyer grew tired of waiting, so the offer went away.

Enter Erin Attardi. She re-listed the home at a compromised price point and a few weeks later, reduced the price to the point where it needed to be to attract a solid offer. The buyer who made the offer was excited about buying the home for the following reasons:

- The home was located in an area with little turnover, which meant there were few homes for sale in this desirable neighborhood.
- The home had a pool, which was a hot button for the buyer.
- The price was under $400,000 in an area where homes sell for a lot more.
- The home appeared to be in great shape.
- There was only one lender, which meant the negotiation time might be short.

The buyer was obtaining an FHA loan to buy this home. Sometimes sellers shrink away from FHA buyers because sellers believe FHA's appraiser may require too many repairs. However, nowadays, FHA guidelines are much more relaxed than they were, say, in the 1990s. FHA approves many loans today, which would not have been approved twenty, even thirty years ago.

Before the home was listed as a short sale, the seller had paid for and obtained a pest report and a pest clearance. Both the report and clearance were submitted to the buyer's lender. The report contained a notation that we often see on pest inspections. It stated there was an inaccessible area under the home that was not inspected. If a pest inspector cannot reach a spot to inspect it, the report will contain that disclosure.

Nobody thought anything about it, and Erin continued to negotiate with the short-sale lender. She was close to obtaining short-sale approval. Escrow sent the HUD-1 to the lender for signature, and the buyer's loan documents were sent to underwriting. Six weeks had passed since the buyer had written the offer. Everything was moving along swimmingly until the underwriter decided the inaccessible area under the home required further investigation. The underwriter insisted that the seller make the area accessible and that the pest inspector should re-inspect.

Because the seller could not pay for any more reports or repairs, the buyer coughed up the $200 needed to open up the blocked area. The pest inspector crawled back under the house. Lo and behold, hidden away in this closed off area was a horde of **powder post beetles**. The revised pest inspection now called for $18,000 worth of repair work, which included tenting the entire home for fumigation.

Erin was at lunch when she heard the news. She immediately dropped her fork, pushed back her pasta plate, and began calling contractors to obtain other bids. By the end of the week, Erin had received four bids, the lowest of which was $10,000. She submitted the $10,000 bid to the short-sale lender, explaining that FHA was now requiring that work to be completed prior to funding.

Another two months passed before the short lender agreed to pay for the eradication of the powder post beetles. If the lender had refused, it would have had to disclose the condition to the next buyer who came along because the FHA buyer would have walked away from the transaction. Many FHA buyers do not put down more than 3.5%. The amount of the post powder beetle work was almost as much as the buyer's down payment, and the buyer did not have the extra money.

After passing this hurdle, Erin thought she and her seller were on the way to closing. What else could possibly go wrong? For starters, the updated preliminary title report now picked up a $3,000 tax lien that had not previously appeared on the report. This was unusual. Generally, title companies are experts at reporting a complete history of the public records that pertain to any property. If the title company misses an item after issuing a title policy, it is on the hook for it. For whatever reason, let's call it human error, the title company missed the tax lien on its original preliminary title report, and since it had not yet issued the title policy, it was not responsible for the lien.

This meant Erin had to go back to the short-sale lender and ask the lender to pay the tax lien. It is not a simple yes or no question because a short-sale lender requires approval from its investors, especially when the deal involves additional funds. The process ate up another six weeks, but the short lender finally agreed to pay the tax lien.

By now, Erin had received three separate short-sale approvals from the lender on this transaction. She was beginning to understand that short sales were not easy, and her first short-sale success was simply a fluke. Erin had listed this home the first week in January, and it did not close until the end of May. Agents who have worked as hard as Erin on these short sales have definitely earned their commissions, sometimes ten times over.

18

Closing the Short Sale

The expression is, "It ain't over until the fat lady sings." In the world of short sales, it ain't over until the short-sale lender signs the HUD-1, submits the short-sale approval letter, and the transaction records in the public records.

A few agents have reported getting to the closing table and finding out the lender has pulled their commission out of the transaction. Can the lender do that? For starters, the commission agreement is between the listing brokerage and the seller, subject to third-party approval. Everybody knows the banks pay the commission, but banks will not sign a listing agreement or commission agreement because they are not the owner of the property.

That means the commission is open for negotiation with the bank. Many banks will discount the agents' commissions, which means it is up to the agents to present a strong case for earning a bigger commission and not just roll over. For example, to attract the attention of a buyer's agent, it sometimes takes a higher commission to get them in the door. Otherwise, there may have been no offer at all. However, once the bank has verbally agreed to the commission, the bank's authorization to pay the commission comes when the bank signs the HUD-1.

The reason a few agents were cut out of their commission at the last minute is because the commission was missing from the HUD-1, nobody noticed it until it was closed, and then it was too late. What can an agent do if the bank refuses to pay commission at the last minute? Agents can submit a new HUD-1 that contains the commission. Agents can maintain a good working relationship with the preparer of the HUD-1, so an omission would be pointed out in advance and not overlooked.

Contrary to popular belief, REALTORS® cannot threaten to cancel the transaction nor take steps to cancel. The first Code of Ethics from the National Association of Realtors says REALTORS® must put the interests of the sellers and buyers above their own and treat all parties fairly. Lawyers argue, and rightly, that to cause a transaction to cancel simply because the agent lost a paycheck violates the Code of Ethics. Therefore, agents must allow the transaction to close because it is in their client's best interests to close the transaction.

In California, our Short Sale Listing (SSL) Addendum specifically states that the payment of commissions is subject to lender approval. If the lender will not cooperate, the broker may cancel the listing. The broker and the seller execute the SSL.

A similar problem that often pops up is the selling broker's commission. Most MLS stipulate that the listing broker must pay the commission offered in MLS as a co-op to the selling broker. Agents who enter listings without verbiage that states the commission may be reduced by the lender and equally divided can find themselves on the hook for paying more than they expected when fees are reduced.

For example, let's say Broker A takes a short sale listing at ten apples and offers to pay any selling broker seven apples. Broker B submits an offer from Broker B's buyer, which is accepted. However, the best Broker A can negotiate with the bank is an agreement to pay seven apples. At the closing table, Broker A offers Broker B three and one-half apples as compensation. Broker A might even take a bite out of the half apple. Broker B has the right to sue Broker A for seven apples, which would leave Broker A with no apples at all.

Lawsuits Happen

Here is an interesting case where a buyer sued the lender for failing to approve a short sale. A buyer, Ribsy Productions, a Solana Beach, CA-based real estate company, sued Aurora Loan Services, based in Littleton, Colorado for reneging on a short sale. The property in question is located in Tucson, Arizona.

According to news reports, Aurora agreed to a short-sale offer of $158,000 on a $587,000 secured loan. That's a 73% drop in the mortgage balance—a big hit for Aurora. Somewhere along the line, Aurora changed its mind and decided to call off the short sale. Therefore, the buyer sued, asking for a suspension of the foreclosure proceedings.

Experts say this case is unlikely to set a precedent. However, for now, it is the only case of its kind.

Procedure for Closing the Short Sale

After the HUD-1 is signed, the seller has deposited the deed, and the buyer's lender has funded, the deal is ready to close.

The seller, by this time, should be packed and ready to move out. Some common contract practices call for the seller to vacate upon recordation at the county courthouse, but possession is always negotiable. Buyers and sellers are wise to compromise and work together to settle on a possession date.

Usually the date of possession is addressed in the purchase contract, but because of the nebulous state of short sales, other terms can override or change the date of possession. A buyer could wait months and then suddenly be informed that the short sale has been approved and closing needs to happen within three weeks. If the contract states possession upon closing, the seller should try to accommodate, but it is not always possible. Rather than beat a seller over the head with the purchase contract, it is far wiser to work out an agreeable arrangement that benefits both parties. You can be right as rain about possession rights, but if the seller refuses to move, you can end up with more problems than bargained for.

What Stays with the Home and What Goes

Fixtures stay with the home. Anything that is physically attached is considered a fixture. The accepted standard in California is M-A-R-I-A. It stands for:

Method of attachment.

Courts have determined that if the method of attachment is meant to be permanent, the item is a fixture. It includes trees, plants, and landscaping affixed to the ground as well.

Adaptability.

If an item has been installed in a specially designed spot, it has adapted itself to the environment. Built-in dishwashers and slide-in stoves fall into this category, as well as carpeting that is installed wall-to-wall.

Relationship of the parties.

If the disagreement is between a landlord and a tenant, the tenant is likely to win. If the disagreement is between a seller and a buyer, the buyer is likely to win.

Intention of the parties.

If the seller intended an item to be a permanent fixture, it cannot be removed. If one installs a spa on a raised deck, connected to plumbing, it is a fixture.

Agreement between the parties.

If the seller agrees in writing to leave the window coverings and later decides to remove the blinds, the seller will lose.

Selling on a short sale does not mean the seller can strip the house or sell built-in appliances. Whether a refrigerator stays or goes depends on if it is specified in the contract. In some states, it is common to take the refrigerator; in others, it is typically left behind. To determine which items may be personal property, read the purchase contract, and talk to your real estate agent.

I always advise buyers to conduct a final walk-through of the premises before closing. Sometimes, I take photographs of the home during the initial home inspection and use these photos as evidence if something is missing. Even if the seller has already moved out and nobody has occupied the home since you last viewed it, always do a final walk-through. The final walk-through is not a home inspection nor is it a time to renegotiate the contract. It is simply a visual inspection to make sure everything is still in working order and that all the items agreed to in the contract are present.

Do not deviate from this practice. I closed a transaction last fall for a buyer who was residing out of the country. Her daughter signed loan documents as an attorney-in-fact. The daughter did not have time to do a final walk-through, so she waived it. The property had been vacant for months, and nobody lived there. A week after closing, the buyer asked if I would do an inventory of the furnishings in the home because the sellers had left all the furniture.

The daughter and I opened the door, and we were immediately hit in the face with a strong odor. It was cat urine. However, we were more distracted by the air conditioning that was left on high at 60 degrees. The place was freezing. There were no labeled controls on the thermostat, no off, on, heat, or cool. It took us a while to figure out how to shut it off.

Within minutes of shutting off the A/C, we heard water running, and it seemed to be coming from the closet. We opened the closet door and water poured out of the air conditioning unit. I quickly grabbed a bucket to catch the water, and we tried to mop up the floor with old towels, but the odor of cat urine was overwhelming. We finally called the home warranty company and asked them to pay a visit. The buyers ended up removing all the carpeting from the home and treating the floor with an enzyme solution—thank goodness it was a slab floor and not hardwood. They were not unduly stressed since they had wanted to replace the flooring anyway, but still. Somehow, a cat must have entered the home unattended.

If we had conducted a final walk-through prior to closing, it is possible that we would have caught this problem and been able to negotiate a settlement from the sellers or held up closing until the sellers remedied the situation. The listing agent claimed she was in the home on the day of closing and did not notice an odor, and the A/C was not abnormal. Therefore, we had no way of knowing whether the condition in which we found the home happened before or after the close of escrow. The point is you never know what can happen, even in a supposedly unoccupied home.

If the sellers have been cooperating throughout the transaction, it is a good idea to ask the sellers to be present during the final walk-through. This way, the sellers can point out all the little things, such as how to jiggle a doorknob to engage the latch or how to work the controls on the spa.

Ask the seller for maintenance records and appliance warranties. Some warranties are transferable to the new owners. When I bought my home, the seller gave me photographs showing where the yard was dug up to install the new sewer line. You will find having these records will be valuable to you down the road.

You might ask the sellers for their new address and/or cell phone number, just in case you have questions later or mail to forward. One question I like to ask sellers is "What is the one thing you've always thought about doing to this home but never got around to doing?" You might be amazed at the answer, and it could be years before you might come up with the same idea.

Change the Utilities

Depending on your locale, you might need to call the utility companies a week or more in advance of when you will actually close. Some utilities have scheduling backlogs, and phone service for a landline could be one of them. Ask your real estate agent to give you a list of phone numbers or Web sites for the electric company, gas company, telephone company, water and sewer, garbage and recycling, newspaper, cable TV company, and DSL providers. If you wait until closing to call, you might find yourself without utilities.

Pick up change-of-address cards or go to usps.com and submit a change of address to forward your mail.

On the day of closing, your agent may meet you at the home to hand you the keys. If you want to be safe rather than sorry, right after the agent hands you the keys, turn around and hand them to the locksmith you have called to meet you. Get the locks changed. Now.

Make the resolution to always pay your mortgage early, never incur a late charge, and thank your lucky stars that you successfully closed a short sale.

What Else Can Happen After Closing?

Ask Frank Wible, a foreclosure specialist at RE/MAX All Pros in Turnersville, New Jersey. Frank said his experience was a first for him. Here is Frank's story:

> *I successfully completed and closed a short sale in February with Countrywide. The process was a nightmare, which took almost six months to get completed, with many complicated issues to overcome.*

I represented the buyer and the seller in this transaction. Although I was able to keep it together, the buyer was frustrated by the time it closed. But, all was good at closing, and they were happy with their purchase.

Come August, the new owner called, freaking out. Why? Because he had found a notice on the door that the home was just sold in a sheriff's sale.

After the call from the new owner, I ran to the office. I pulled the file and reviewed everything; it was all fine. I called immediately Countrywide. After reviewing the documents with the person on the phone, we discovered the loss mitigation representative reversed a digit in the account number on the approval letter and closing instructions. So, OK, how can this get fixed?

Here's the thing, that loss mitigation representative and his boss no longer worked at Countrywide. The account we had wired the money to was a Bank of America account (we closed right in the middle of the merger), and the person I had on the phone was clueless about how to solve the problem. The highest person I could reach was a regional director, who also had no idea what happened nor what to do about it. I was told they would start an investigation, like an investigation was going to immediately solve the situation. I was beside myself, thinking, ***what was I going to tell this homeowner tonight?***

The research department finally found the money and the problem. The problem was the loss mitigation representative put an "8" instead of a "9" in the account number when B of A sent the approval letter. It was credited to the mortgage of a guy in Las Vegas. A simple keystroke error from the loss mitigation negotiator created a huge mess in the system.

I guess it proves that they are, in fact, human after all.

The issue was not that it happened, but what it took to clear it up. I must have talked to ten or more people just to get to the root of the problem. No one knew what to do, or how to resolve the problem, not even management!

To date, Countrywide is claiming it was not its issue, and that the mistake had come from a third party who typed the letter. Even when it makes obvious mistakes, Countrywide seems ready to blame someone else. Also, it was not willing to put in writing that the transaction had been reversed and no further action would be taken against the home. We contacted Countrywide's lawyer on this case, who confirmed that all items have been resolved . . . however, Countrywide's lawyers would not put that promise in writing either!

The good news, if any, is that the new homeowner invited me over for drinks and dinner, claiming that what I did for him went well over and above the call of duty! Knowing I helped someone is the best and only reward I need!

Apparently, the situation that happened with Frank's new homeowners is common. A forum member identified as

"NoKnowledge" on my homebuying site at About.com posted a similar experience in September of 2008. The member said two months after her son and daughter-in-law bought a home, the sheriff showed up on their doorstep with an eviction notice. The sheriff declared the couple could not possibly have purchased the home since it was in foreclosure! Either the sheriff had the wrong address, or the bank made a clerical mistake.

An Indiana homeowner was almost locked out of her home due to a bank's mistake stemming from her purchase of a short sale. Channel 6 News in Indianapolis reported in September of 2008 that Janet Perkins had bought a short-sale home, closed in August, and was busy painting and fixing up her new home when a company representing Citibank showed up to change the locks. They kept telling her to vacate the premises, but Perkins insisted she owned the home. Turned out that one department at Citibank forgot to inform another department that the property was sold.

The smart thing to do is to put a copy of your HUD-1 and deed in a safe place and be ready to produce it, should a bank's representative or a sheriff show up at your house after closing.

19

Short Sale Experiences from the Pros

Evelyn Johnston, a real estate agent with Prudential One Realty in Elkhart, Indiana, shares a heartwarming story about how she sold her first short sale as a new agent. A family we will call the Madisons owned the home. The Madisons bought this five-bedroom, five-bath on five acres five years ago. Mr. Madison held two jobs at that time, and his wife traveled for business. Together, they had no problems paying their $3,800 mortgage payment, until they faced a medical emergency.

After injuring his back, Mr. Madison was hospitalized for three weeks. The stress of seeing her husband in the hospital and in such pain caused Mrs. Madison to experience an epileptic attack, and then she was hospitalized for two weeks. Once the Madisons fell behind on their mortgage payments, they could not catch up. They tried to make partial payments and work with the bank. However, Mrs. Madison's doctor put her on medication and suggested she find an inside job with less stress. After Mrs. Madison quit her high-paying job and settled into retail sales, the family could not continue to make their mortgage payments and fell even further behind.

Here is Evelyn's experience:

In Sept of 2007, I received a sales lead from our Prudential One Realty in-house referral program. I called the customer and set up an appointment to see an REO property. I was a new real estate agent and forgot to ask ahead of time about the preapproval letter, so I had no idea if they were qualified or not to buy a home.

When we met, the Madisons really liked the home, and they really liked me. We wrote an offer on the spot. They told me they had their home listed for sale and already were wishing that I was their listing agent. At the time, it didn't dawn on me that they might need to sell to buy this REO. Nevertheless, I called the REO agent to say I had an offer on the property, but unfortunately, it was already under contract with another buyer.

I showed the Madisons other homes for a couple of months, but nothing really grabbed their interest, until I showed them a short- sale property. While touring the short-sale home, the Madisons took me into their confidence and admitted that they were in the same predicament. My heart went out to them.

After their listing expired in December, I was the obvious choice to list their five-bedroom home. I outlined my marketing plan ahead of time and showed them what I would do differently to sell their home. The Madisons agreed to all my strategies and signed on the dotted line. Over the next several weeks, we adjusted and adjusted the price until we started getting interest. When we hit the right price point, we suddenly had forty-three showings in fewer than thirty days.

The Madisons were becoming exhausted from accommodating all the buyers who were traipsing through their home, but even with that much activity there were still no offers. Finally, we dropped the price one more time and immediately received an offer! This was the point where my work really began.

The mortgage company—which shall remain nameless—is a very large mortgage company, maybe the largest in the country, and I had heard horror stories about working with this company. They were all true. Every customer service agent I spoke with gave me a conflicting story, the sheriff's sale date was looming, and I couldn't tell if anything was being done. At one point, I counted the number of people I had spoken to and it turned out I had engaged in conversations with fifty-seven different employees at the mortgage company.

I met with the appraiser, and after I knew he had mailed the appraisal to the short-sale lender, I started calling every day. No matter what they said—such as they wouldn't know anything for thirty days after the appraisal was received—I still called daily to get the next person's take on the situation. Two months later, the mortgage company said I had an acceptable offer, and a negotiator would be calling me later that day or, at the very least, the following day. The person who approved the short sale asked me questions and calculated the loan payoffs as we spoke.

The next day when I called, I was informed that we had nothing. No approval, nothing. Unfortunately, I had already called the selling agent who in turn had called the buyers with the happy news. I couldn't believe what I was hearing now. I called back and connected with yet another customer service agent, and he said the same thing: there was no approval. My heart sank.

I asked to talk to a supervisor, but the rep discouraged me by saying the supervisor would not be able to tell me anything more. After an extended period on hold, the customer service rep came back to the phone to say that although the supervisor was busy, the supervisor had managed to sneak a peek at the file. Sure enough, a negotiator had been assigned; however, that person was on the phone. I kept the customer service rep on the phone talking until the negotiator was available to speak with me.

The negotiator said she would review the offer, but it was not accepted at this time. I dreaded having to pass along this recent development to the selling agent, but I picked up the phone and called him to share the news that I had no real news. His buyers, to put it mildly, were furious, and I didn't blame them. They demanded to meet face-to-face. I agreed to meet with them and explained what had happened.

After we met, the buyers seemed to understand what had transpired. Then, several hours later, I received a very nice call from the buyers. They said they were glad I was working so hard to get them the home they have always wanted. It was their dream home. I was very relieved.

But the clock was ticking. It wasn't until the evening before the sheriff's sale that I received word the sheriff's sale had been canceled. Talk about sitting on pins and needles. Then, a week later, I received a verbal acceptance. Just like that. Two weeks from then, I received the short-sale approval letter and, at long last, we closed.

I originally listed this home for sale at $359,000, and the Madisons dropped and dropped the price until it hit $210,000; we settled for $224,000 cash. By the way, the Madisons and I are best friends now. I feel like my real success was the fact that I was able to place them in a home under a 3.5-year lease purchase agreement. They are very happy and cannot wait to own this home as soon as possible. Their home sold, the mortgage company forgave their debt and promised to report to the credit bureau that their loan was paid agreed for less than amount owed (a charge-off).

This story has a happy ending. The Madisons sent Evelyn a letter after it closed. Here is what the Madisons had to say

All I can say is we just connected with Evelyn. From the moment we met her, it was like being with a member of the family that we hadn't seen in a while. Although she was professional in her manner, what showed up to us the most was that she cared about meeting our needs. Not just selling us a house. Since we have gotten to know her better, we know we were exactly right . . . When my father-in-law passed away, Evelyn was right here, fixing us dinner. She truly is a member of our family!

In case you think only lower-priced homes sell on short sales, Wendy Rulnick, a real estate broker at Rulnick Realty in Destin, Florida, says upper-end homes are just as vulnerable to a short sale. She calls this next story **My Best Real Estate Deal on the Emerald Coast:**

I received a pleading telephone call in November of 2007 from an agent at another real estate company. The agent represented a seller whom she felt she could no longer represent. The seller was facing foreclosure and wanted to do a short sale to hopefully lessen the impact on his credit and his self-worth. Although the agent had diligently tried for six months to sell this home, she did not want to handle a short sale and she had no short-sale experience. So, she referred the seller to me.

This was a waterfront home on the Santa Rosa Sound in a higher price range—a range that wasn't selling very quickly at this time of year. The seller owed about $750,000.

What was this homeowner's story? Truly, his was one of the most heartbreaking short-sale hardships I have ever encountered. The seller, who had fared better a few years earlier, had bought his family's dream retirement home in Florida. A little more than a month after he closed, Hurricane Ivan hit the Gulf Coast. Ivan all but demolished his home.

The cost to rebuild added an extra $250,000 to his mortgage. He invested two years in the search to find a contractor who could repair his home. He could not sell his primary home while rebuilding the Florida home, and he soon exhausted all his life savings by keeping the payments current on both homes. On top of this, his income had dropped by two-thirds and then, to compound matters, his wife had transplant surgery. He was seriously depressed and confided, "I am not the man I was."

After sixty days, I received notice that the foreclosure sale was scheduled for the end of January, only a few weeks away. We had been frantically dropping the price like a fall from a skyscraper while I continued full force with my marketing efforts. By a miracle, we received an offer on a Friday before the scheduled foreclosure sale that Monday.

Over the course of the previous several weeks, we had dropped the price from $799,900 down to $539,900. The offer we received was 489,000. I scrambled to get the fifty-one-page fax ready to go to the bank with a foreclosure stop order request.

I called the bank twenty times. They refused to put me through to loss mitigation. I left message after message to stop the foreclosure sale. I faxed numerous times pleading for a stop order. By 5:30 PM, the bank's general mailbox delivered an outgoing message that it had now closed. I was exhausted. I had no assurance they would look at this offer and stop the foreclosure. There was nothing else I could do over the weekend.

First thing Monday morning, though, I called the bank. I had little hope remaining. Guess what? The bank postponed the 11 AM foreclosure sale and placed a thirty-day hold, pending review of the short-sale offer.

Two weeks later, the bank approved the offer as a short sale. I cannot begin to tell you the relief in my seller's voice and the gratitude in his heart when I called to report that we had short-sale approval, and his foreclosure was called off. The seller wanted to repay me—he was so delighted. In reality, my true payment was the fact that this was the most fulfilling work I have ever done.

Another Florida Realtor, Katerina Gasset, at International Properties and Investments in Wellington, has a different take and swears that persistence pays off. Even when it looks the bleakest, miracles can still happen. Even when faced with stupidity, Katerina and her husband Nestor marched on. Here is Katerina and Nesterís frustrating short-sale experience:

The call came in from an expired letter my husband, Nestor, regularly sends out. When listings expire, we write to the sellers and offer to sell their home. The seller on the other end seemed dismayed, and frustration filled his voice. In a cynical fashion, he made it clear that he doubted that we could help him with his short sale because he had already spent countless hours on the phone with his lender. He initially had hope of working out some kind of solution and, on all fronts, his lender had turned him down.

Well, we don't like to lose. Nestor will bite into the deal and not take no for an answer. As reluctant as he was, the seller decided to give it one more chance. He had invested in a condo project that had gone bad and filed bankruptcy to protect him from the backlash of the real estate market downturn. By this time, he was in foreclosure. Most of the time, we communicated through his son who was a partner in one of the condos. The beginning of this short sale was one of little faith on the part of the sellers.

Nestor priced the property at market value, and we received an offer soon thereafter. No one was anticipating the extent of the negotiating that would ensue. The offer was for $169,000.

A major real estate lender serviced the loan, but the note was owned by Freddie Mac. A BPO was ordered. We received a call from a real estate agent from Fort Pierce, Florida—an hour drive from the subject property. This out-of-area agent knew nothing, absolutely zero, about this property or the condo development. Nestor was armed with comparable sales for this condominium and offered to help the agent prepare his BPO. The agent selected comparables from outside of the condo development and appraised the seller's condo at $239,000, when we had one of the exact same models under contract at $155,000. We had listed this condo at $169,000 because that's what it was worth.

As a result, the bank's negotiator called to say the bank expected to net $218,000! Yeah, right! Nestor talked until he was blue in his face to get the nego-

tiator to understand it was a grave mistake to carry that kind of expectation. No buyers in their right mind would buy a condo with market values dropping like flies at a price like that.

After spinning our wheels with the negotiator, we took the matter directly to Freddie Mac. Nestor filed a complaint with Freddie Mac contesting the erroneous BPO. We struggled through a lot of red tape and were finally able to persuade Freddie Mac to order a review of the goofy BPO. But they hired the same real estate agent who prepared the first BPO to review his own work. How smart was that? Now that two months have passed, the real estate agent produced a new value of $169,000.

The problem was sales prices had by now fallen even more, plus, the buyer grew tired of waiting and had withdrawn his offer. At this point, closed MLS sales were between $145,000 and $155,000. The BPO was still way off in left field.

Even though we received offers at $145,000 and $150,000, the short-sale lender still turned them down because it now wanted a price based on the revised BPO of $169,000.

Fortunately, although the sellers were in foreclosure, the lender did not want to foreclose. Again, we crawled up the ladder at Freddie Mac and complained. This time, we sent in every single offer and additional evidence that the BPO was wrong.

In the meantime, we received an offer of $135,000, all cash. We sent the all-cash offer to the bank, ex-

plaining that all the other buyers had given up and walked away. We said the bank can either foreclose or take this offer because the prices were going to continue dropping, which would have meant they would have received even less as time goes on.

Finally, Freddie Mac listened and ordered a third BPO. This time they hired an agent who lived in the area, who knows and understands our market.

Within a week, we received a fax with the short-sale acceptance at the all-cash offer price of $135,000. This short sale took months and months to finally get approved. In retrospect, if the bank had acted quickly and decisively in the first place, it could have received $169,000. Its delay and failure to process this short sale appropriately cost it $34,000.

The sellers were stunned when we called to congratulate them for finally having closure in this chapter of their lives.

The moral of the story is that to service clients, agents must never give up. Even if an agent is working in the red, it is a short-sale listing agent's obligation to help sellers prevent foreclosure. The reward is happy clients.

To say the sellers were happy is as if saying a fat cat on his back in the sun is happy. They sent Katerina and Nestor a follow-up letter:

You have rescued us from a very bad position in what may be the worst real estate market since the Great Depression, and we will forever be grateful...Thank you, thank you, thank you, we cannot thank you enough for all of your hard work and tireless efforts.

Your knowledge, skill, marketing efforts, professionalism, and, most important, your pit bull-like tenacity, I believe, are the reasons for your success. In a profession where many are only looking for the easy sale and the Big Commission check, you both proved that you are not just in it for the money but that you truly care about your customers and are not afraid of hard work to get a property sold.

I would say that is one happy client! Count 'em, two. Congratulations, Nestor and Katerina.

A common occurrence that I have been hearing repeatedly has come from agents who sold a home and did not find out until it was under contract that it was actually a short sale. This can happen for several reasons, such as the home was not worth what the seller and agent initially thought it was worth, so it sold for less than the loan amounts. However, in the next story, a second mortgage popped up out of nowhere and threw the agent's listing into short-sale status.

Roland Woodworth, a realtor at Exit Realty, Clarksville, Tennessee, successfully closed a surprise short sale after a five-month struggle, which he calls his most challenging transaction. Here is his story:

I first met my seller in October of 2007 and, at that time, his mortgage payments were in arrears. However, when I finally secured the listing the following February, the seller claimed he was current on his payments, and this would definitely NOT be a short sale.

If we sold at list price, the seller would break even. So, I took the listing as a regular listing. Over the next sixty days, we had many showings and then came the offer we had been waiting for. After negotiations, we had a ratified contract and proceeded to the closing, just like a regular transaction. Everything was smooth as silk.

However, two days before closing, I received that call from the title company that no agent ever wants to receive. The title company found a junior lien recorded against the property. I don't know how or why the seller forgot to mention this to me, but obviously, the seller had no money to bring in to pay off that loan. After recovering from the initial shock that we were not going to close on schedule, I realized that the only way to close this deal was to submit it for a short sale.

I was not prepared for the saga that followed. First, I called the first mortgage holder to let that bank know this would be a short sale. Next, I attempted to track down the second mortgage holder. Talk about a tangled, twisted mess. When I called the company listed on the title search, the phone was answered with a different company name. I explained who I was and sent my authorization form, which allowed the company to release information to me. Needless to say, this company did not want to negotiate and demanded the full amount. To make matters even more confusing, its beneficiary demand was issued on yet another different letterhead. That's when I figured out that the second mortgage holder was actually part of the first mortgage company but a collections department.

About forty-five days later, I received a settlement letter from the first mortgage company, which includ-

ed a dollar figure it was willing to give to the second mortgage company. We had made progress, and I was happy, thinking all I needed now was the short-sale demand letter from the second mortgage company, and we would close. But, no.

Instead, the second mortgage holder transferred the file to its attorney for collection. I called the lawyer and explained what had happened and how we wanted him to cooperate with a short sale. The lawyer didn't care about the short sale. He claimed he was hired to file litigation against the homeowner, and that's what he planned to do.

I pretty much ran around in circles for the next forty-five days, calling the second mortgage holder and its lawyer, getting no results. Finally, I called the account manager and was told the short sale would be approved. Great, I thought, now we will close. But, no.

Now, we had to wait for a new approval from the second mortgage company, and their contact person was unavailable. After several days of spending hours holding on the phone, I managed to get the e-mail address of the account manager. This proved to be the best thing because now I could document the madness. Several more weeks passed without results. By this time, I literally begged for assistance from both mortgage companies.

The shortsale negotiator for the first mortgage company was very helpful and enlisted her manager's help using my paper trail. After countless phone calls and e-mails, I received the call we had all been waiting for—the second mortgage holder was now ready to settle the account. Except it wanted 10% of the balance, which was more than the first mortgage holder had approved.

This meant I had to go back to the first mortgage company and renegotiate. At least, the first mortgage company was more reasonable than the second, and it agreed to adjust its short-sale approval letter to make the transaction work. So, now, I figured, we were ready to close. But, no.

The reason we couldn't close this time, however, had nothing to do with the mortgage holders. It's because the seller had an ex-wife whom the title company insisted must sign a quitclaim deed. So I tracked down his ex-wife and got the deed signed. OK, we must be ready to close now, right? But, no.

Turned out the seller had remarried during this long and agonizing process, which meant his new wife had to sign the deed conveying title to the new buyers. This wasn't nearly as difficult to do after jumping all those other hurdles. I got the new deed signed, and we closed, five months after we had gone under contract. If I am ever faced with another situation like this, at least now I will be prepared and know what to expect.

In our last story, Chris Ann Cleland, a realtor at Long & Foster in Braemar, VA, learned the hard way that some short sales could go on for a year. Chris Ann is an experienced short-sale agent who never expected a short sale to take this long. Over the years, she figured out how to expedite files and get answers from even the most reluctant negotiators but dealing with this particular transaction made her question her sanity:

I met a couple I'll call the Kellys in October of 2007. Mr. Kelly had recently succumbed to a devastating illness. As the breadwinner of the family and unable to work, he was collecting disability, which was about half of his former salary. Relying on disability for support meant he could no longer afford to pay his mortgage payments, especially in light of compounding medical bills. When the Kellys realized they were headed for foreclosure, they called a friend who introduced them to me.

Unfortunately, the builder was still selling homes in this subdivision, and none had gone on the market as a resale. This was a two-bedroom, two-bath home in a newer Active Adult Community for people over the age of fifty-five. The HOA dues were very steep, more than $500 a month, and included just water, basic cable, and an Internet connection.

This would not be an easy sale in a better market, and the market of 2007 was still declining, making my job that much more difficult. On top of the soft market conditions, the builder was still cranking out buildings and new units. And, as builders often do, they were leveraging anything and everything to entice buyers to sign on the dotted line. The builder offered incentives such as two years of HOA fees, all the buyers' closing costs, two years' subscription fees for an alarm system, and a golf membership within the community.

Since the Kellys were facing no other choice but foreclosure, we started the ball rolling to market this home as a short sale.

The first thing I did was alert the lender, Countrywide, to the potential short-sale situation by making phone calls and faxing the standard required documentation such as the hardship letter and listing agreement. Countrywide held two loans on the property: a first and second mortgage. We listed the property on November 1, 2007, with the bank's blessing. Keeping a close eye on the builder's sales progress, we made price reductions along the way. We started at $259,000 and made reductions, landing at $225,000, $218,000, $199,000 and had to come all the way down to $175,000 to finally compete with the builder and get buyers through the door.

The Kellys and I had started negotiations for a deed in lieu of foreclosure in November when the listing hit the market. We knew this would be a tough sale with the age restriction and exorbitant monthly fees. I employed a trick I had used on other Countrywide short sales. When sellers initiate negotiation for a deed-in-lieu, Countrywide immediately orders an appraisal and title work, which can then be transferred to the short sale upon receipt of a purchase offer. That way, most of the hard work was done. After an offer was received, all that was left to do was get a negotiator and wait for a response from the investors.

After missing seven months of mortgage payments, on May 29, 2007, the Kellys received an offer while at *the $175,000 list price. The offer was $170,000. Hooray! I was confident my deed-in-lieu trick had already put us ahead of the game. I quickly assembled a comparable market analysis, which reflected the recent sales by the builder, including incentives. Our closest competing home was brand new construction, which had sold for $202,000. After the incentives were deducted, that new home sale actually resulted in a net sales price of $185,000.*

Compared to that home, the buyers' offer for Kellys' short sale at $170,000 looked reasonable, so we sent the offer, along with the standard required documentation. We overnight expressed the hard copy of the contract package and, to cover all my bases, faxed the package, too. It took a week before it was logged by Countrywide as received.

With two appraisals already completed by Countrywide, we were confident that we would be on the fast track. I called Countrywide every day, talking to the lower-level gatekeepers in their phone cue. Each time I called, I explained that we had two valid appraisals and requested an assignment to a short-sale negotiator. I received a different response from each employee that answered my call: 'No ma'am. We can't assign a negotiator until we order ANOTHER appraisal." Or "Yes, you are in the cue for an appraiser." I made notes of every conversation, for whatever good that would do.

By late June, Countrywide ordered a third appraisal. Why? You tell me. We had two valid appraisals that had not yet expired, but Countrywide's employees were evidently informed that they could not deviate from standard operating procedure. By early July, Countrywide had not yet received its third appraisal. Meanwhile, we still had no negotiator assigned to the file because, a month later, the third appraisal was not yet received.

When the third appraisal finally arrived, it did not take into account the tens of thousands of dollars the builder gave as incentives to buyers, so it wasn't really a valid appraisal nor did it reflect accurate value. I felt like I was banging my head against the wall, except it didn't feel any better when I stopped banging. It was like being on a merry-go-round with no way to jump off. We asked for another appraisal.

By the end of July, that fourth appraisal had been submitted and we were now, two months later, officially assigned a negotiator. The negotiator's response was to counter the buyers' offer at $185,000. This would have been a semi-reasonable counter offer two months ago, but the market had declined even further by now. The buyers held firm with an offer of $170,000, and the negotiator informed us that he would send the offer to the investors on the loan—the now infamous Fannie Mae.

Let me stop here and say that it is absolutely no surprise to me that Countrywide had to be bailed out by Bank of America, or that the folks at Fannie Mae drove their company right into the ground, needing resuscitative efforts by the government.

I waited a few days to follow up with the negotiator and called. Nothing. No response. I left messages for three days straight. No response. When the negotiator did respond, he was totally oblivious about our previous conversations and correspondence. I inquired about the response from the investors and was informed: "I have not sent the contract to the investors, and won't, until I hear back from you regarding the counter offer of $185,000."

I nearly fell to the floor. Thank goodness, I had kept our written correspondence. I faxed him the documents that showed he had agreed to send the offer based on the buyers' decision to stand firm at their original offer of $170,000. Hours later, he admitted his mistake but that didn't save the two weeks we had wasted. The buyer's loan lock had already expired and, after an extension, was set to expire again.

So now, the offer is off to the investors, Fannie Mae. I saw the light at the end of the tunnel. Fannie Mae, with four appraisals (written evaluations of price by a licensed professional) decided to order a Broker Price Opinion (BPO). A BPO compared to an appraisal is like asking a person sitting next to you in a doctor's waiting room what is wrong with you. Truly an asinine move, in my opinion.

After another month of waiting and calling everyday to check status, we heard back from our negotiator. Fannie Mae had a counter offer to the contract. Mind you, the contract was barely beneath market value when we started, and we had gone through three months of *declining values coupled with an increase in builder incentives—incentives that Fannie Mae and Countrywide would never agree to and the buyers did not demand. The counter offer? $215,000. Yes. That's right. Fannie Mae, in its infinite wisdom, countered ABOVE what the builder was offering for NEW and included no incentives. Of course, the buyers declined.*

Enter the phase of a short sale I didn't even know existed until then—the reconciliation phase. This is when the buyer hires a professional to do an appraisal and submits it to Countrywide, which then submits it to Fannie Mae. Luckily, the buyers' lender had done an appraisal in late June, and we submitted it the very same day to our negotiator. Ta-da. Done deal.

Yeah, right, only in my dreams.

I called. No response. Sent an e-mail. No response. Another two weeks passed by, and the negotiator asked me why I was corresponding with such urgency. He said his hands were tied until he received the buyers' appraisal, which we had sent two weeks ago. It's like déjà vu—another two weeks of correspondence that landed in the bucket of hell. So, I sent the appraisal again and sent a copy to the negotiator's supervisor, including a copy of the two-week old e-mail where I had originally attached the appraisal.

Ah . . . another apologetic phone call from the negotiator. "So sorry for the miscommunication. This will be in review with Countrywide for seven to ten days before it will be sent to Fannie Mae."

All right. At least we know we're in the home stretch. I call daily from day 5 to day 14. On day 14, I received a hardly cordial reply from an employee in the "phone queue" who told me that my point of contact had changed. I now had a brand new negotiator who was waiting for me to send the fourth appraisal.

I was thinking, "Is this like the movie Groundhog Day? Am I being punked?" By a miracle, the original negotiator finally confirmed that he had the buyers' appraisal and was sending it over. Are you with me here? You might be wondering, as I was, what is going on at Countrywide? How was I supposed to know my point of contact changed? Did anybody call? "Ma'am, that is not our responsibility to inform you when we change your point of contact." Were they serious?

So I yelled and screamed and got a supervisor. The very next day, our new negotiator had the appraisal and finally submitted the file to review with Countrywide.

But wait, then the new negotiator called to say that Fannie Mae would need yet another BPO with the contract. Not this again! Why not open a window and ask people on the street what they think of the offer?

That was last week. This is now a year later, and I am at the end of my rope. Who knows if this property will go to settlement? Meanwhile, the sellers have missed eleven mortgage payments and are harassed multiple times daily, as am I, by the Countrywide collections department. The right hand has no idea what the left hand is doing. Meanwhile, the buyers have had to extend the interest rate lock on their loan four times! It's a miracle they are still waiting.

And this seems like a good place to end this book.

Contributors to The Short Sale Savior

Erin Attardi, executive associate, Lyon's Sierra Oaks office
2580 Fair Oaks Blvd , Suite 20, Sacramento, CA, 95825
(916) 342-1372, email: Erin@erinattardi.com

Chris Ann Cleland, Realtor, Long & Foster
7526 Limestone Drive, Gainesville, VA 20155
(703) 402-0037, email: chrisann@longandfoster.com

Pacita Dimacali, agent, Gallagher & Lindsey Realtors
2424 Central Ave, Alameda, CA 94501
(510) 205-2992, email: Pacita@PacitaRealtor.com

Katerina Gasset, Realtor, International Properties and Investments in Wellington
1021 Cherry Lane, Wellington, Fl, 33414
(561) 502-1577, email: Katerinag@bellsouth.net

Evelyn Johnston, real estate agent, Prudential One Realty
1741 E Bristol Street, Elkhart, In, 46514
(574) 304-7148, email: evelyn@evelynjohnston.com

Wendy Rulnick, real estate broker, Rulnick Realty
12889 Emerald Coast Pkwy, Ste. 107-A, Destin, FL, 32550
(850) 259-0422, email: itswendy@rulnickrealty.com

Frank Wible, foreclosure specialist, RE/MAX All Pros
5701 Route 42 South, Turnersville, NJ, 08012
(856) 745-7700, email: fwible@comcast.net

Roland Woodworth, Realtor, Exit Realty
1289 Northfield Dr, Ste 3, Clarksville, TN, 37040
(931) 278-2207, email: rolandwoodworth@topproducer.com

About the Author

Elizabeth Weintraub has an extensive background in real estate spanning more than 30 years, including experience in related industries such as title and escrow. She is a full-time broker-associate at Lyon Real Estate's downtown Sacramento office and is recognized as a top producer. She is also a member of the Master's Club, a production level bestowed by the Sacramento Board of Realtors and has earned Senior Executive Associate status at Lyon Real Estate.

Elizabeth began in the business in 1974 as a title searcher at First American Title in Boulder, Colorado. Moving to Newport Beach, California, she became an escrow officer in 1976 and advanced to certified status, as designated by the California Escrow Association. By 1979, Elizabeth obtained her real estate broker's license, bought the company she worked at, and opened branch offices of Real Estate of America in Orange County.

Elizabeth moved back to Minnesota in 1991 to be near family. She bought, fixed up, and sold homes in the Midwest before returning to California in 2002.

She joined Lyon Real Estate in 2003 and lives in Land Park, Sacramento, with her journalist husband and three cats.

LaVergne, TN USA
08 April 2010
178550LV00003B/158/P

9 781574 723762